Automating Media Centers and Small Libraries

Automating Media Centers and Small Libraries

A Microcomputer-Based Approach

Dania Bilal Meghabghab
Valdosta State University

1997
Libraries Unlimited, Inc.
Englewood, Colorado

LIBRARIES UNLIMITED, INC.
P.O. Box 6633
Englewood, CO 80155-6633
1-800-237-6124
www.lu.com

Constance Hardesty, *Project Editor*
Sheryl Tongue, *Design and Composition*

Library of Congress Cataloging-in-Publication Data

Meghabghab, Dania Bilal, 1956–
    Automating media centers and small libraries : a microcomputer-
based approach / Dania Bilal Meghabghab.
    xxvii, 172 p. 19×26 cm.
    Includes bibliographical references and index.
    ISBN 1-56308-472-4
    1. Small libraries--United States--Data processing. 2. Small
libraries--United States--Automation. 3. School libraries--United
States--Data processing. 4. School libraries--United States--
Automation. 5. Instructional materials centers--United States--
Data processing. 6. Instructional materials centers--United
States--Automation. 7. Microcomputers--United States. I. Title.
Z678.93.S6M43   1997
025′ .00285--dc21   97-6249
                                                           CIP

*I dedicate this book to my loving father, Mustafa,
and mother, Yusra. To my husband, George,
whose encouragement and support have resulted
in the writing of this book.
To my siblings, nieces, and nephews.*

Contents

Figures

Tables

Foreword

Dania Meghabghab's guide for automating media centers and small libraries is long-awaited by educators of media specialists and practitioners in the field. Most of us have had to collect a number of documents covering various aspects of automation before we could begin to make sense of the process and visualize the steps we would need to take before a completed online catalog would be in use in our library or media center. This volume explains the process step by step for librarians and media specialists starting to automate, or wishing to update or migrate to another automated system.

In a concise style, Meghabghab starts with the process of identifying and prioritizing the library's or media center's needs; this encompasses a variety of tasks, from information access to control of the materials. Her final two chapters cover OPACs on the Internet and the future of OPACs.

Meghabghab's underlying theory is that selecting a microcomputer-based automation system should be based on preliminary screening and preview of existing automation software, needs assessment, a choice of an operating system, platform, and budgeting. The lists of specifications she has included for the various functions that many libraries and media centers want are extensive, and provide excellent examples to follow in creating a request for proposal. Vendor responses should give the reader considerable information for decision making.

Preparing the library or media center shelflist for automation is a step that many people think of first in the automation process. However, its power to affect the process is more evident with its placement in Meghabghab's discussion of implementation. Throughout her explanation of U.S. MARC records creation, she gives us the means to understand why this part of the automation process is important and provides the foundation for everything that follows. Her discussion of shelflist analysis and conversion of MARC records through various options is knowledgeable and complete. Along with an explanation of the advantages and disadvantages of each option, Meghabghab's inclusion of a cost analysis for the varied options is particularly eye-opening for librarians and media specialists with administrations convinced that using local resources and personnel would save money.

Finally, this work contributes to the reader's understanding of the importance that online public access catalogs (OPACs) will have in networked information access. Through her insightful analysis, the reader will see a vision of each media center's and small library's place in the school building, the surrounding community, and the world. Of importance is the inclusion of the Z39.50 standard. Media specialists and librarians should be cognizant of Z39.50 and what it does for the profession. Meghabghab's discussion is both timely and essential.

I am personally excited about using this volume with my students who are graduate students at the University of Georgia. This is a process-oriented volume that should make a strong contribution to the understanding of automation.

Julie Tallman, Ph.D.
Department of Instructional Technology
University of Georgia

Acknowledgments

I wish to thank Drs. Catherine Price, head of the Department of Curriculum, Instructional Technology, and Secondary Education, and F. D. Toth, dean of the College of Education, Valdosta State University, for granting time from my partial teaching duties to write this book. I also extend my thanks to the students I taught in IT 755 (Technology for Automating Media Centers) during 1996 for field testing partial chapters of this book and for recommending activities. Special thanks are offered to students Chantell Stonecypher and John Karew for their invaluable feedback and comments. Grateful acknowledgment is given to Rick Morgan, technology specialist, Educational Technology Training Center, Valdosta State University, for serving as a referee on chapter 7 and for sharing his expertise in networking. Many thanks are extended to Dr. Julie Tallman, associate professor, Department of Instructional Technology, University of Georgia, for writing the foreword.

Thanks are also extended to Susan Zernial, Libraries Unlimited acquisitions editor, Stacey Chisholm, Libraries Unlimited author relations coordinator, and Constance Hardesty, editor, for their assistance during the writing of this book.

Introduction

An automated system combines both software and hardware. The software consists of a computer program designed to perform various library functions, such as circulation, cataloging, public access, acquisitions, and serials control.

The hardware comprises input devices (e.g., keyboard, mouse); output devices (e.g., printer, monitor); central processing unit (i.e., microprocessor); main storage (i.e., main memory); secondary storage (e.g., floppy diskettes, hard disks); and communication devices (e.g., modems, Integrated Service Digital Network [ISDN]). Software and hardware must work concurrently and properly to run an automated system.

Software designed for automation can operate on three categories of computers: mainframes, miniframes, and microcomputers. The first category is suitable for large academic, research, and public libraries with millions of titles in their collections. The second category is appropriate for medium-sized libraries with collections of more than 300,000 titles. The third category is recommended for all types of small libraries, such as media centers, corporate libraries, medical libraries, and public libraries with smaller collections.

Small libraries differ from large and medium-sized libraries in terms of their collection size, mission, number of patrons they serve, level of staffing, funding, and the need for software and hardware for automation. Although the general automation process can be applied to most libraries, media centers and small libraries require a special approach. For example, a media center with limited financial resources may resort to converting library records using in-house original cataloging instead of a CD-ROM database of MARC records, or it may contract with a commercial vendor (e.g., Follett, Winnebago, Brodart) instead of a bibliographic utility, such as the Online Computer Library Center (OCLC).

The general similarities among small libraries pertain to the low number of professional staff (i.e., one or two) and limited financial resources. The differences lie in their mission, type of clientele, kinds of services, and collection. The mission of a media center, for example, is to provide information access and services that meet curriculum, educational, and recreational needs of students, teachers, and staff.

A public library's mission is to render access to information and services to all people to meet their educational, informational, recreational, and cultural needs. The mission of a medical library is to furnish an up-to-date research collection and information services that meet the immediate needs of its clientele. Central to these services, for example, is access to online databases (e.g., Medline) available through commercial vendors, such as DIALOG; this service is not provided by many media centers. Additional differences may pertain to priorities for automating library functions. A medical library may rank the automated serials function as one of its top priorities because of the extensive periodical routing performed within the organization. A public library with branches may consider automated acquisitions a high priority because of its centralized material purchasing and processing. A media center may regard the circulation function as the highest priority for automation because of the intensity of routine tasks involved and the heavy demand for the service. Regardless of the priorities for automation, however, all small libraries may find microcomputer-based integrated automated systems appealing. This is due to the development of software designed to suit the needs of various types of small libraries. Unison, from Follett Software Company, and Winnebago, from Winnebago Software Company, for example, are suitable for media centers and public libraries. Inmagic, from Inmagic, Inc., is appropriate for special libraries.

■ Filling a Gap in the Literature

The lack of texts that describe the automation process in a simple, systematic manner, taking into consideration the unique characteristics of media center programs and the unique needs of small libraries, led to the writing of this text. During the last four years I have taught automation for media specialists in the instructional program at Valdosta State University. To do this, I had to gather information from many sources and design activities and projects to provide students with the knowledge and skills they need to carry out an automation project. No single source of appropriate information and activities was available.

In 1992, when I started to teach the subject, I relied on Catherine Murphy's *Automating School Library Catalogs: A Reader* (1992), which I supplemented with other materials. Murphy's collection of essays and articles is not intended as a textbook or a guide for automating media centers; hence some topics are not covered.

Keith C. Wright's *Computer-Related Technologies in Library Operations* (1995) is the most recent text about automating media centers. The book covers various functions that can be automated. Although the book is a helpful guide, it lacks information about application of U.S. MARC/MicroLIF Protocol, networking, database maintenance, the Z39.50 standard, hardware configurations for automated systems, issues related to information retrieval, access to online catalogs in cyberspace, and hands-on activities.

Automation for School Libraries: How to Do It from Those Who Have Done It, edited by Teresa T. Day, Bruce Flanders, and Gregory Zuck (1994), is a collection of essays intended to provide model procedures and basic facts about automating a small library, based on the experiences of librarians who have done it. It is a valuable book but is best used as a supplemental reading rather than a guide or textbook.

The gap in the literature demands a work that can be used as a textbook for graduate students in library automation as well as a guide for practitioners who are involved in an automation project. Educators of library and information science who teach automation will find this text provides a systematic explanation of the whole spectrum of processes involved in automation, including

> planning and needs assessment;
>
> choosing and configuring suitable hardware;
>
> system selection and implementation;
>
> writing requests for proposals;
>
> retrospective conversion, including cost analysis for various retrospective conversion options and specifications;
>
> application of bibliographic standards (e.g., U.S. MARC/MicroLIF Protocols);
>
> barcoding;
>
> networking; and
>
> making online public access catalogs (OPACs) accessible via the Internet.

In addition to explaining the processes involved in automation, the book covers issues in information retrieval and provides hands-on activities.

☐ Goals of This Book

The main purposes of this work are to furnish the reader with a textbook and guide that provides them with knowledge and understanding of

> the overall process of automating media centers and small libraries;

the various steps involved in automating media centers and small libraries;

the concepts pivotal to automation and networking;

bibliographic standards central to automation and networking;

the role of the Z39.50 standard in providing access to OPACs in cyberspace;

the various components, topologies, and architecture of a local area network (LAN);

the main issues affecting end-user information retrieval in OPACs;

the roles that media specialists, information professionals, software vendors, and system designers play in improving access to OPACs; and

the skills needed to apply certain automation processes.

The last is accomplished through the hands-on activities that appear at the end of most chapters.

The main focus of this book is on automation using minicomputers. Automation using minicomputers or mainframes, and issues related to joining bibliographic utilities (e.g., OCLC), are beyond the scope of this book.

■ Organization of the Book

This book is divided into nine chapters. Chapter 1 provides a brief overview of the development of OPACs and the standard U.S. MARC/MicroLIF Protocol, which is the bibliographic standard for the import and export of cataloging records that identify specific materials. Chapter 1 also covers the benefits and pitfalls of library automation.

Chapter 2 discusses preparing for automation. Essential first steps are knowledge acquisition and needs assessment. Knowledge acquisition means learning about automation; the reader is pointed to a number of resources, including journals, trade shows, and experienced colleagues, for more information about the topic. Needs assessment involves analyzing functions and tasks using charts or work-flow patterns, as well as gathering quantitative data about each function in order to justify its automation. The chapter offers several lists of items that should be considered before one decides whether or how to automate and before writing any vendor requests. This part of the process can be time-consuming, but it is vitally important to understanding how and where the automation system should be used to create the most benefit. The last step in needs assessment is analysis and interpretation of the collected data, which helps one determine priorities for automation. To facilitate needs assessment, the chapter details a step-by-step approach to data gathering, analysis, and interpretation. Finally, chapter 2 makes the point that automation is not performed to save money. Rather, it is performed to improve media center or library services; enhance access to the collection; and increase productivity, accuracy, and efficiency. The chapter ends with an activity that allows readers to practice various processes involved in needs assessment.

All information professionals, including media specialists, are (or shortly will be) affected by automation to some degree. Therefore, all must be aware of the various types of computer systems (microcomputers, miniframes, and mainframes), as well as the options for configuring the hardware, for automated systems. Chapter 3 briefly describes microcomputers and three common hardware configurations for microcomputer-based automated systems. The characteristics and the advantages and disadvantages of each configuration are discussed.

Chapter 4 discusses the system selection process, focusing on the selection of an integrated microcomputer-based automated system. The chapter describes the selection process, provides guidelines for preparing a request for proposal (RFP), and presents a sample RFP. The sample RFP covers essential specifications for the whole system as well as for each library function, including utilities, circulation, OPAC, cataloging, authority control, acquisitions, and serials. Sample specifications for hardware (e.g., a file server) are described. Although the software specifications are extensive, it is not possible to create one list of specifications that will apply to every library or media center; the specifications must be tailored for each automation project. Managers of an automation project may want to develop additional specifications and delete some of the ones included in the example. In addition, many of the specifications considered essential in chapter 4 may be considered only desirable in some libraries or media centers. Managers must adapt the specifications to suit the needs and requirements of each media center or library. This chapter concludes by listing a few pitfalls to avoid during the selection process.

Chapter 5 delineates the various stages and activities related to preparing the collection for automation. This process involves weeding, inventory, and shelflist analysis. Database creation, which is accomplished through retrospective conversion (Recon) of the shelflist, is described in detail. This discussion covers the various options for accomplishing Recon, the method of achieving each option, and the advantages and disadvantages of each option. Of most importance is the cost analysis of vendor versus in-house Recon options; this comparison shows the high cost of the latter. In addition to the overview of Recon, chapter 5 provides essential specifications for the process, regardless of the conversion method used. These specifications can also be used for ordering MARC records from book vendors.

Chapter 5 also covers barcoding the collection and using bibliographic standards pivotal to automation, such as the *Anglo-American Cataloguing Rules, Second Revised Edition* (*AACR2R*; Gorman and Winkler 1988) and *International Standard Bibliographic Description* (ISBD). It also describes in detail each component of the U.S. MARC/MicroLIF Protocol record.

Other processes important to implementation, including site preparation, which includes selection and placement of hardware, printers, and furniture; system installation and testing; computer security; and end-user instruction for OPAC are described in chapter 6.

Crucial to this chapter is a discussion of the process of database maintenance, which covers the most important fields, such as the Leader, fixed field, author field, title field, subject headings fields, added entry fields, and record filing. An activity about database maintenance is included at the end of this chapter.

Networking the media center or library—that is, connecting a set of computers to form a local area network (LAN) for the purpose of sharing software and hardware peripherals, such as printers—has become common. Chapter 7 presents a brief overview of the process of networking. It covers various types of LANs and describes the advantages and disadvantages of each. The three main components of a network (i.e., cabling, topology, and architecture), as well as considerations in installing cables, are discussed. A brief description of wireless LANs is also given. The LAN topologies (i.e., bus, star, and ring) are illustrated to present the variations among them. In addition, the three most common LAN architectures (i.e., Ethernet, Token Ring, and Fiber Distributed Data Interface [FDDI]) are described. The chapter lists selected companies that supply networking products. An activity about networking is included at the end of this chapter.

The Internet is transforming media centers and libraries into virtual hubs of information. The number of OPACs on the Internet is increasing rapidly; media specialists and information professionals must learn to use this powerful information tool. Chapter 8 discusses methods for making OPACs available via the Internet. In addition, it includes brief descriptions of accessing OPACs in cyberspace and touches on the importance of the Z39.50 standard. It also covers the most important benefits of OPACs' presence in cyberspace.

Chapter 9 postulates that OPACs have progressed from replicas of a card catalog to a powerful information tool. It is critical that media specialists and information professionals learn about the problems that end-users are currently experiencing in accessing OPACs, and that they become involved in solving these problems for future OPAC users. The chapter describes the progress OPACs have made during the last 15 years, addresses problems related to access, and offers some ideas for addressing those problems. The key question is: Will OPACs survive the digital revolution? The answer is yet to be determined.

☐ Activities

A total of seven activities are included in this book. These activities have been field-tested by students in a class called Technology for Automating Media Centers. Educators may modify the activities to suit the needs of their students.

■ A Note on Terminology

Three terms have special meaning as they are used in this book. They are:

> *Media specialist* is used for *school library media specialist.*

> *Information professional* is used to refer to practitioners in small libraries other than media centers.

> *Library* indicates the small library.

■ References

American National Standard Institute and National Information Standards Organization. 1995. *American National Standard Information Retrieval Application Service Definition and Protocol Specifications for Open Systems Interconnection.* (ANSI/NISO Z39.50.) Bethesda, MD: National Information Standards Office.

Day, Teresa T., Bruce Flanders, and Gregory Zuck, eds. 1994. *Automation for School Libraries: How to Do It from Those Who Have Done It.* Chicago: American Library Association.

Gorman, Michael, and Paul Winkler. 1988. *Anglo-American Cataloguing Rules, Second Revised Edition.* Chicago: American Library Association.

Murphy, Catherine. 1992. *Automating School Library Catalogs: A Reader.* Englewood, CO: Libraries Unlimited.

Wright, Keith C. 1995. *Computer-Related Technologies in Library Operations.* Brookfield, VT: Gower.

1 Overview of Automated Systems

■ There are two types of automated systems: stand-alone and integrated. A stand-alone system includes one or more modules that represent library functions (e.g., circulation or cataloging and public access) that do not share a common database. An integrated system is a suite of interrelated modules that perform a variety of library functions (e.g., circulation, cataloging, public access, acquisitions, and serials) and share a common database.

■ Modules and Their Functions

Public access, or the online public access catalog (OPAC), is what users consult to find and retrieve information of interest. Generally, OPAC is equivalent to the card catalog, but it provides advanced search features. The OPAC function allows searching by author, title, subject or keyword; searches using Boolean logic; and combined search strategies, for example, author–title or author–subject. The OPAC module is the only one that is inseparable of cataloging. A library cannot have OPAC without the cataloging module, because the cataloging module is the database that houses all material records and makes them available in OPAC. Therefore, the cataloging module is the heart of the automated system.

The cataloging function is accomplished in the cataloging module. This module performs various cataloging tasks, such as original cataloging using the Machine-Readable Cataloging (MARC) and the Microcomputer Library Interchange Format (MicroLIF) protocols, editing, copying, saving, and retrieving cataloged records. When a record is saved in the cataloging database, the record automatically appears in OPAC, and a brief copy of the record is also generated automatically for the circulation module.

The circulation module performs the tasks involved in the circulation function, such as material check-in, check-out, inventory, overdue notices, holds and reserves, fines, and interlibrary loan.

1

The acquisitions function is performed in the acquisitions module. It includes tasks, such as material requests, purchase orders, material receipt, budget, and record keeping.

The serials function is achieved in the serials module. It covers tasks such as periodical subscription, acquisitions, routing, claiming, cancellation, and record keeping. For details about the features of each module, see chapter 4.

The circulation, acquisitions, and serials modules function separately in a stand-alone automated system, but they may operate both separately from and with each other in an integrated automated system. The module that is common to all functions, in both integrated and stand-alone systems, is the utilities module, which is used for management (e.g., to prepare and generate statistical reports) and for customizing the software (e.g., to change the screen color or select MARC fields for keyword indexing).

□ Integrated Modules Versus Stand-Alone Systems

An integrated automated system is preferred over a stand-alone system, even when one module is purchased at a time. In an integrated system, as modules are added over time, the modules will share one common database and interface with one another. This interface provides users with improved services. With an integrated system that includes modules for circulation, OPAC, cataloging, acquisitions, and serials, a user

---

The Automation Marketplace

The microcomputer-based automation marketplace is growing rapidly. The decline in the cost of hardware and software, the continuous augmentation of software search features, the capabilities of software to interface with sources like CD-ROM databases and the World Wide Web, the implementation of the Z39.50 standard, and the increased availability of software in Macintosh, DOS, Windows, and Windows NT platforms will continue to make microcomputer-based automation software appealing to many small libraries. In 1996 Barry, Griffiths, and Peiling reported that 64 percent of all microcomputer-based automated systems licensed were for school libraries, 16 percent were for special libraries, 15 percent were for public libraries, and 3 percent were for academic libraries. These statistics indicate that media centers dominate the microcomputer-based automation marketplace.

Based on 1995 sales, the most popular microcomputer-based systems are Follett Catalog Plus, Circulation Plus, and Unison; Winnebago Circ/Cat, Brodart Precision One, Companion Alexandria, and Data Trek Graphical Library Automation System (GLAS) Professional Series and Management Series; Inmagic Inc.'s Inmagic, and the Library Corporation Bibliofile Cataloging, Bibliofile Circulation, Bibliofile OPAC, and Bibliofile ITS for Windows cataloging software (Barry, Griffiths, and Peiling 1996).

who locates an item of interest in OPAC can obtain the bibliographic information and the call number. The user can also determine the status of the item (i.e., check-out date, due date, and whether the item is missing or withdrawn)—a service provided through the circulation module. In addition, the user can ascertain whether the item being searched in OPAC is on order, received, or in processing—a service provided through the acquisitions module. When a patron is looking for a certain issue of a periodical in OPAC, the patron is informed whether the issue is received, claimed, canceled, or sent to the bindery—a service provided through the serials module.

A media center or library with limited financial resources may acquire one module at a time. This decision must be based on the media center's or library's priorities for automation.

■ Online Catalogs

The introduction of online public access catalogs (OPACs) to libraries has made a marked impact on the way users access, retrieve, and manage information. This powerful information-retrieval tool has allowed media specialists and information professionals to provide more effective and efficient information services.

Online catalogs were introduced in the 1960s by large university and public libraries. The software packages were developed by the libraries' in-house staff and operated on mainframe computers. During the 1970s and 1980s, turnkey automated systems (i.e., systems that are commercially available with preconfigured hardware and software) and software designed to operate on existing library hardware emerged. Mainframe- and miniframe-based systems that dominated the market during that period were, because of their high cost, beyond the reach of many media centers and small libraries.

> The term *online catalog* refers to the whole software. The term *OPAC*, or *online public access catalog,* is commonly used to refer to the public access module. The two terms are also used interchangeably.

The proliferation of microcomputers in the early 1980s provided an incentive to automate media centers and small libraries. Computer Cat, an Apple II microcomputer-based online catalog, was the first automated system to be introduced in a media center. Developed by Colorado Computer Systems in 1981 for Mountain View Elementary School in Colorado, the system comprised three main components: OPAC, cataloging, and inventory (Costa 1981, Costa 1982). Computer Cat OPAC was a replica of the card catalog; it allowed users to search by author, title, and subject.

In 1985, only 130 school sites implemented stand-alone circulation and catalog systems (Murphy 1988). During the next few years, microcomputer processing and storage capacity increased while the price of hardware plummeted. This provided a unique opportunity for vendors to develop automation software. Integrated microcomputer-based automated systems that supported single and multi-user configurations and that combined multiple functions (i.e., OPAC, cataloging, circulation, acquisitions, and serials) were introduced before the end of the decade.

☐ The Breakthrough in Automation

In 1987, a breakthrough in microcomputer-based automation occurred with the development of the bibliographic standard Microcomputer Library Interchange Format (MicroLIF). This standard was developed by a committee of system and book vendors. The purpose of MicroLIF is to import MARC records into microcomputer automated systems using floppy diskettes and to allow the exporting of MARC records. MicroLIF proved to be incompatible with U.S. MARC. Among other problems, MicroLIF lacked a directory, an essential element in a MARC record. (The directory indicates to the computer the MARC tag, field length, and the starting character position of each field [Byrne 1991].) In 1991, system and book vendors introduced a new MicroLIF standard that conformed in its entirety to U.S. MARC. The new standard became known as U.S. MARC/MicroLIF Protocol.

The 1990s have witnessed an escalation in implementation of microcomputer-based automation systems. Based on a survey of 1993–1994 expenditures of selected school libraries, Miller and Shontz (1995) found that 64 percent of the respondents used microcomputer-based automated systems for circulation, 76 percent used them for overdues, 61 percent for inventory, 60 percent for cataloging, and 34 percent for acquisitions. In 1995, media centers dominated the automation market with almost 64 percent of total sales (Barry, Griffiths, and Peiling 1996). This increase can be attributed to:

- Decrease in the cost of software and hardware
- Increase in storage capacity and processing
- System conformity to U.S. MARC
- Expansion in search capabilities
- Ease of use and user-friendliness
- Support of various networking platforms (e.g., Novell Netware, Microsoft's LAN Manager, Apple Macintosh LAN) and operating systems (e.g., MS-DOS, Microsoft Windows, Macintosh, and UNIX)

- Availability of affordable CD-ROM databases to use for in-house retrospective conversion (e.g., Bibliofile, Precision One, Alliance Plus)

- Accessibility of integrated systems that combine circulation, cataloging, OPAC, acquisitions, and serials-control functions

- Ability to interface online catalogs with CD-ROM databases, the Internet, online databases, and other application software (Meghabghab 1994)

■ Benefits of Library Automation

Every library, regardless of the type and the size of its collection, benefits from automation. What is most evident about automation is that it improves library services and increases productivity, efficiency, and accuracy in performing a variety of library operations. Additional benefits of library automation are:

- It allows patrons to use search strategies that exceed those that can be used with card catalogs. Card catalogs can be searched only by author, title, and subject; OPACs can be accessed by author, title, subject, and keyword. In addition, users can extend their search by using Boolean operators (i.e., *and, or, not*) and by combining search strategies (e.g., title and author, subject and author). In addition, OPAC users may limit their search results by such features as publication date, type of material (e.g., magazine, book, video), language, or reading level, and they can sort bibliographies by author, title, and publication date.

- It allows patrons to search the library's collection from locations outside the library's walls. Patrons who are equipped with a computer and a modem can dial into the OPAC from home, office, or other remote location.

- It provides users with timely access to library materials. Library materials can be placed on the shelves as soon as items are processed and U.S. MARC/MicroLIF Protocol records are downloaded into a database. This eliminates the need for time-consuming original cataloging.

- It supports new means of information retrieval by introducing patrons to global information. The popularity and success of OPACs make them ideal to interface with CD-ROM databases, online databases, the Internet, bibliographic utilities (i.e., Online Computer Library Center [OCLC], Georgia Online Database [GOLD]), and other information systems. Users feel competent using OPAC for information retrieval or as an online searching tool.

- It eliminates routine tasks or performs them efficiently. The circulation function, which includes check-in, check-out, overdue notices, and inventory (to name only a few of its functions) is tedious, repetitive, and time-consuming. In her 1986 research, Nancy Everhart found that in a nonautomated environment it took 30 minutes to check in 50 items, 4 hours to compose overdues, and 1 hour to generate a monthly circulation report; that compared to 5 minutes, 15 minutes, and 10 seconds, respectively, to perform the same tasks in an automated environment. With the advancement of computer technology, these activities are performed at a much faster speed.

- It expedites and simplifies the inventory of library materials. The automated inventory is performed by scanning each item's barcode using a hand-held device, downloading scanned items into the automated system, and generating a variety of customized reports. In a nonautomated environment, this procedure involves taking a shelflist drawer to the stacks to be inventoried, matching each shelflist card against the respective item on the shelf, flagging the shelflist cards for missing items, and generating an inventory report. The collection inventory that takes two months to complete in a nonautomated environment may take two weeks or less in an automated environment.

- It encourages cooperative collection development and resource sharing (e.g., interlibrary loan). Automated media centers and libraries can develop a union catalog and join bibliographic utilities.

- It enables media centers and libraries to import and export U.S. MARC/MicroLIF records. Records (i.e., records obtained from book vendors or other sources on disk) are imported into an automated system to save cataloging time. Records can be exported from one system to a new automated system without incurring new costs for retrospective conversion.

- Integrated systems that support material acquisition, serials management, budget administration, and record keeping reduce the amount of time spent on these functions.

- It motivates patrons, equips them with problem-solving and information-retrieval skills, and provides them with lifelong learning experiences.

- It reinforces a positive attitude about the media center or library and improves the image of the media specialist or information professional. Patrons view the media center or library as an indispensable place for gaining access to information and consider the media specialist or information professional a powerful information provider.

■ Disadvantages of Library Automation

Despite the many benefits, library automation also has the following disadvantages:

- It is time-consuming. Planning, selecting, implementing, networking, and managing an automated system requires a significant, long-term commitment of staff time.

- It is costly. Start-up costs, such as record conversion, software, hardware, networking, cabling, and wiring; ongoing expenses, such as software updates, supplies for printers, barcode labels, annual maintenance, and technical support; and subscription to or leasing retrospective conversion databases may be more than many media centers and small libraries can afford.

- The demands of the automated system may not leave staff enough time to provide new services or to work with students, teachers, and other clients. In fact, automation eliminates some tasks but generates new ones. End-user training, ongoing troubleshooting of hardware and software, and database maintenance place new demands on the media specialist or information professional.

- Access to the automated system is unavailable during system downtime. This may cause frustration for both users and media specialists or information professionals.

Awareness of the benefits and pitfalls of library automation will help media specialists and information professionals better prepare for the changes in their work duties. Automation is, like any technology, costly in terms of time and money, and frustration and anguish are typical symptoms of technostress.

■ References

Barry, Jeff, Jose-Marie Griffiths, and Wang Peiling. 1996. Jockeying for supremacy in a networked world: Automated system marketplace 1996. *Library Journal* 121 (April): 40–51.

Byrne, Deborah J. 1991. *MARC manual: Understanding and using MARC records.* Englewood, CO: Libraries Unlimited.

Cibberalli, Pamela R. 1995. IOLS software: Options for school libraries and media centers. *Proceedings of the Tenth Integrated Online Library Systems Meeting,* New York, May, pp. 21–33.

Cohn, John M., Ann L. Kelsey, and Keith M. Fields. 1992. *Planning for automation.* New York: Neil-Schuman.

Costa, Betty. 1981. Microcomputers in Colorado—It's elementary. *Wilson Library Bulletin* 55 (May): 676–717.

———. 1982. An online catalog for an elementary school library media center. *School Library Quarterly* 10 (Summer): 337–46.

Everhart, Nancy. 1986. *MMI Preparatory School computerized model library.* ERIC Document ED 291389.

———. 1994. How high school library media specialists in automated and nonautomated centers spend their time: Implications for library educators. *Journal of Education for Library and Information Science* 35 (Winter): 3–19.

Meghabghab, Dania Bilal. 1994. Automating school library media centers in Georgia: A survey of practices and knowledge. *School Library Media Quarterly* 22 (Summer): 221–30.

Miller, Marilyn Lea, and Marilyn L. Shontz. 1995. The race for the school library dollar. *School Library Journal* 41 (October): 22–23.

Murphy, Catherine. 1988. The time is right to automate. *School Library Journal* 35 (November): 42–47.

Saffady, William. 1994. *Introduction to automation for librarians.* Chicago: American Library Association.

———. 1991. *Automating the small library.* Chicago: American Library Association.

2 Preparing for Automation

Automation involves a spectrum of activities that is much broader than selection and implementation of a system. To prepare for the automation project, media specialists and information professionals should identify the mission and goals of the host organization as they relate to the media center or library, acquire adequate knowledge of the automation process, develop an understanding of various library functions, assess staff needs and user information needs, and examine the sources of funding for the automation project.

Media specialists and information professionals who are engaged in an automation project must possess adequate knowledge about a wide range of issues, including

evaluating, selecting, and implementing an automated system;

software and hardware terminology;

automated systems' functional specifications;

users' information needs; and

the various operations of the media center or library.

The important things to learn are:

- The benefits and pitfalls of library automation.

- The impact of automation on the organizational structure in general and on the media center or library in particular. Such impacts may include access to the online catalog from offices and other locations within the organization; the kind of services that may be eliminated, redefined, or created; changes in staff responsibilities; and the need to create new positions and eliminate or redefine existing positions.

- Issues and problems related to users' information-seeking behavior when using online catalogs. Studies have shown that users experience problems in searching online catalogs (Hirsh and Borgman 1995; Wildemuth and O'Neill 1995; Solomon 1994; Kilgour 1991; Jacobson 1991; Chen 1991; Kuhlthau 1991; Edmonds, Moore, and Balcom 1990). Being aware of these problems helps one to select an automated system that helps users avoid the most common mistakes and difficulties.

- The features of the most popular microcomputer-based automated systems. Because the automation marketplace changes from year to year, seek the most recent information. Consult the annual April issue of *Library Journal*, the biannual *Directory of Library Automation Software, Systems, and Services,* and *Library Technology Reports,* a periodical devoted to the evaluation of library automated systems, library systems, equipment and supplies. The Librarians Information Online Network (LION) Web site (http://www.librarynet.org/~lion/lion.html) also provides useful information. LION is an information resource for K-12 librarians; it covers comprehensive resources related to automation and other subjects.

- Background information about each of the most popular automation systems, including the modules available, the modules that have recently been added, and the strengths and weaknesses of each module.

- General historical background and financial information about the companies that support the most popular systems. The financial stability of the companies is especially important.

- The automated system vendor's present and future efforts in implementing new technologies, such as supplying Internet-access software compatible with the online catalog, providing cross-platform applications (i.e., Macintosh and PC), and implementing systems that will operate across a variety of platforms (e.g., DOS, Windows, Windows NT).

- Each automated system's profile and its suitability for media centers, special libraries, or small public libraries; its strengths and weaknesses in general; its networking platform (i.e., Novell for PCs and AppleTalk for Macintosh), its compliance with U.S. MARC/MicroLIF protocols, and its rating based on reviews.

■ Knowledge Acquisition

Learning about automation will reduce the many risks involved in automation (Sliveke 1991). One can learn more about automation by researching the library literature. "The Automated System Marketplace," an annual column appearing in the April 1 issue of *Library*

Journal, as well as various issues of *Library Technology Reports,* are good places to start.

Library Journal's April issue includes an annual survey of automated systems for various types of libraries. The April 1996 article by Barry, Griffiths, and Peiling covers the most popular microcomputer- and minicomputer-based automation software, discusses trends and developments in software, and describes the automation marketplace. It also profiles vendors and their products and provides their postal addresses and Internet addresses. *Library Technology Reports,* a periodical devoted to the evaluation and rating of automation software, library systems, library equipment, and supplies, provides comprehensive evaluations of various types of software.

For additional, detailed descriptions of various types of software, consult the *Directory of Library Automation Software, Systems, and Services,* compiled and edited by Pamela Cibbarelli (1996). This biannual directory describes and compares microcomputer, minicomputer, and mainframe software packages. It also provides detailed analysis of each package, such as software and hardware requirements, compatibility with bibliographic standards, components, applications, search features, and price.

☐ Learning from Colleagues

Communicating with colleagues (in person or via listservs, such as LM_NET) to ask for advice or to share successful—and unsuccessful— automation experiences will provide insight into the strengths and weaknesses of selected automated systems. Subscribing to technology-

---

Finding Colleagues on the Internet

Listservs (mail lists) and newsgroups (bulletin board-type discussions) are two ways you can converse with colleagues on the Internet. For a comprehensive listing of listservs and newsgroups consult the LION home page (http://www.libertynet.org/lion/~lion.html).

Listservs

Association of Educational Communications and Technology (AECT): Listserv@wvmvn.wvnet.edu

International Association of School Librarians (IASL): iasl-link@rhi.hi.is
Library and Information Science Forum: JESSE@UTKVM1.UTK.EDU
Library Media Specialists Forum (LM_NET): Listserv@listserv.syr.edu
Special Library Association Discussion List: Listserv@listserv.sla.org

Newsgroups

Deja News (http://www.dejanews. com) is the major World Wide Web site for searching for newsgroups.

oriented mailing lists or newsgroups is another good way to learn from the experienced and the expert. If possible, it is a good idea to form a partnership with a nearby library that has recently undergone automation; this will allow you to learn about the experienced library's successes and failures.

☐ Learning at Conferences and from Vendors

People new to automation should attend workshops or sessions at conferences to learn the basics about automation. Attending vendors' product review sessions at state and national conferences allows one to preview software packages. Early in the preparation process, such previews will help you to understand the various features that automation has to offer. Later in the process, after some software packages have been selected for consideration, you will preview those software packages on site. At that point, inviting companies to provide demonstrations of their automated systems will clarify the systems' functions and capabilities and thus help you to evaluate automated systems. Learning about software features is not enough, however; you will also want to research the companies' financial stability, service, products, reliability, and experience. Automation companies may go out of business, shift their priorities from automation, or sell their software to other companies.

■ Needs Assessment

Needs assessment is the second step in preparing for automation. It is conducted to analyze and evaluate the current media center's or library's services, procedures, and functions in order to improve productivity, effectiveness, and efficiency. It is also conducted to assess staff and user needs.

☐ Staff Assessment

Most people reject change, even when the need for change is obvious (Havelock and Zlotolow 1995). People resist change because of uncertainty, fear of losing control, and concern about performing new tasks or fulfilling new duties competently. Managers of the automation project should strengthen their leadership skills, develop an understanding about change, and assume the role of the change agents whose task it is to provide support and create an environment that lowers the barriers to change. Coping with change may require redirecting personnel and financial resources, because "Library automation and declining budgets [may cause] the redistribution of the library workload" (Oberg 1995) and, therefore, result in an increase in paraprofessional positions and decrease in professional ones. An assessment of staff will reveal their concerns, their current roles and responsibilities, their level of job satisfaction, and their openness to change. It will provide a framework for defining existing problems, diagnosing future problems, reevaluating job descriptions, and reassigning responsibilities.

Staff involvement is crucial to the success of an automation project. Well-trained staff can assist with many tasks, such as needs assessment, data collection, shelflist preparation, and collection inventory, among other things. Staff should be provided the opportunity to acquire the necessary knowledge of the automation process.

Because automation affects all staff, it is important that they be involved in the decision-making process. This involvement will reduce job insecurity, foster confidence in performing new activities, and garner staff support. It is recommended that staff be included on the automation committee. (The need for an automation committee is discussed below.)

☐ Users Assessment

Users include students or clients, administrators, teachers, and other staff. A needs assessment survey of users will indicate their information needs, their concerns about automation, and possible problem areas that need to be addressed.

☐ Role of the Automation Committee

It is recommended that an automation committee be formed. The automation committee is responsible for planning and coordinating the automation project from start to finish. This includes data gathering, needs assessment, researching the literature, attending conferences and seminars, preparing the media center or library for automation, developing a Request for Proposal, evaluating proposals, and selecting and implementing the automated system.

The committee should include representatives from staff and users, as well as media specialists and information professionals. The chair of the committee may report to or work with the technology coordinator or other personnel that oversee the operation of the media center or library.

☐ Questions to Ask in the Needs Assessment

Understanding the mission and goals of the media center or library in relation to those of the host organization is an integral component of needs assessment. Some questions to address during the assessment process are:

> What are the host organization's present and future technology priorities?

What are the media center's or library's present and future technology priorities?

What media center or library services and procedures can be improved through automation?

How will automation increase media center or library staff productivity, accuracy, and efficiency?

Are there alternatives to automation that may equally improve services, procedures, and productivity?

Automation is time-consuming and costly. Engaging in an automation project requires a long-term commitment of staff and financial resources. Clarifying the goals and objectives of the media center or library at the outset is essential to avoid unnecessary expenditures. As Wright (1995) maintains: "No library can afford to indulge in activities which cost money and take staff time unless these activities are directly related to library goals and objectives" (p. 9).

The needs assessment process includes function analysis, data gathering, and data analysis and interpretation.

☐ Function Analysis

The first step in a needs assessment is to analyze each existing media center or library function. Typical functions include circulation, cataloging, information retrieval, acquisitions, and serials. Each function and task should be analyzed and evaluated in relation to the procedures used to accomplish it.

The circulation function includes material check-out and check-in, overdues, fines, inventory, reserve, renewal, and report management.

The cataloging function involves cataloging a variety of items in-house or ordering preprocessed catalog cards when items are purchased. (When in-house cataloging is performed in a nonautomated setting, catalog cards may be produced on premises, or they may be purchased.)

The public access, or information retrieval, function provides service to patrons to meet their information needs. These needs can be met by using the catalog or other bibliographic tools available in the media center or library.

The acquisitions function involves item verification prior to ordering, supplier identification, purchase order preparation, fund encumbrance, item receipt, invoice verification, fund adjustment, and report management.

The serials function includes check-in, routing, claiming, accounting, and report management.

To develop a clear understanding of the procedures involved in each function, it is useful to draw and compare two diagrams of the most important workflow patterns—one workflow diagram showing how the procedure is accomplished in a nonautomated environment and one diagram showing how it is accomplished in an automated environment. (For examples, see figures 2.1–2.6, pages 16–18.)

☐ Data Gathering

The second step in needs assessment is gathering quantitative data about each function; this information is used, first, to justify the automation of each function and, second, to set priorities for automating the various functions. Tables. 2.1–2.5 (pages 19–23) illustrate guidelines for data collection. To apply these schemes in gathering data, decide whether to collect the data on a weekly, monthly, or annual basis and use a check mark to indicate the appropriate category. As applicable, provide the number of operations for each task (based on the workflow diagram); the time spent performing the task; the frequency, or how many times the task is done in the time period you selected (weekly, monthly, or annually); and the accuracy, preferably expressed as a percentage, of accomplishing the task. If a criteria does not apply to a task, write N/A (not applicable), in the appropriate cell. Calculate the total or average number of activities or tasks, the time it takes to achieve them, frequency in performing them, and accuracy in completing them.

☐ Data Analysis and Interpretation

The final activity in the needs assessment is analyzing the collected data in relation to the workflow patterns. This analysis will allow you to determine which functions to automate, and in what order to automate them. Prioritizing the functions to be automated allows one to effectively allocate financial resources. This is especially important when a media center or library is experiencing budget constraints, because it allows the media center or library to reap the greatest results from its investment in automation.

Typical questions to ask in determining priorities are:

Which tasks are the least productive?

Which tasks are the most repetitive, labor-intensive, and time-consuming?

Which tasks result in inaccuracy, inefficiency, and ineffectiveness?

Text continues on page 24

Figure 2.1 Circulation function: Nonautomated item check-out task.

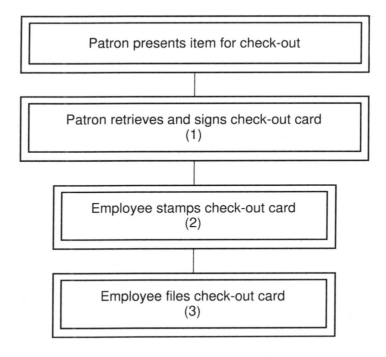

Figure 2.2 Circulation function: Automated item check-out task.

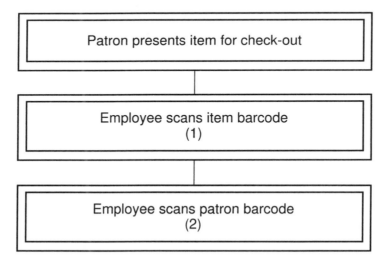

Figure 2.3   **Circulation function: Nonautomated item check-in task.**

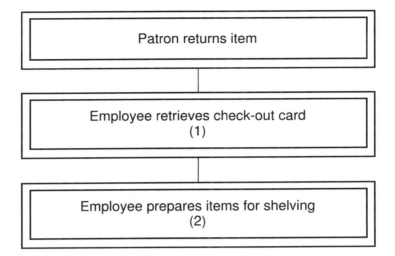

Figure 2.4   **Circulation function: Automated item check-in task.**

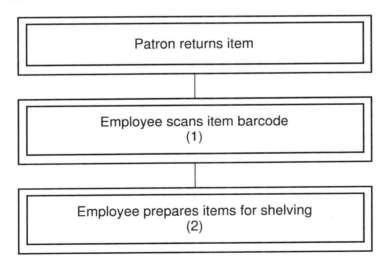

Figure 2.5 Circulation function: Nonautomated inventory task.

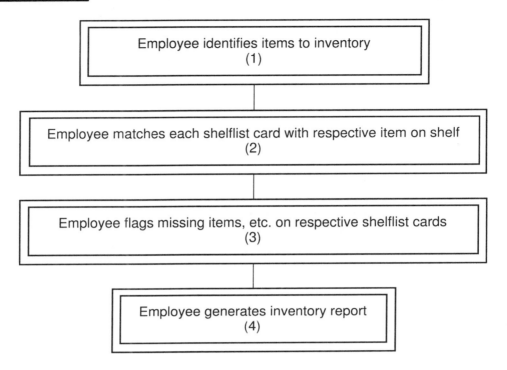

Figure 2.6 Circulation function: Automated inventory task.

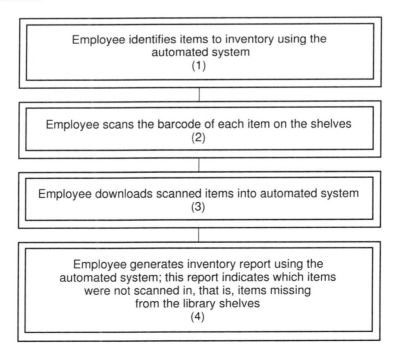

Table 2.1   Data Gathering Scheme for the Circulation Function

Weekly_____   Monthly_____   Annually_____

Tasks	Number	Time	Frequency	Accuracy
Item check-out				
Item check-in				
Overdues and fines composed				
Reports generated for overdues and fines				
Item inventory preparation				
Inventory report generated				
Item check-out card filed				
Item check-in card filed				
Backlogs in card filing				
Item reservation/hold processed				
Item reservation/hold notices sent				
Equipment booking processed				
Equipment booking notices sent				
Other tasks:				
Total/Average				

From *Automating Media Centers and Small Libraries.* © 1997. Dania Bilal Meghabghab. Libraries Unlimited. (800) 237-6124.

Table 2.2 **Data Gathering Scheme for the Cataloging Function**

Weekly_____   Monthly_____   Annually_____

Tasks	Number	Time	Frequency	Accuracy
Print item cataloged in-house				
Nonprint item cataloged in-house				
Catalog card produced in-house				
Preprocessed catalog card ordered				
Cost of preprocessed card orders determined. Write cost in parentheses. ($)	N/A	N/A	N/A	N/A
Backlogs in cataloging		N/A	N/A	N/A
Card filing in the catalog				
Other tasks:				
Total/Average				

From *Automating Media Centers and Small Libraries*. © 1997. Dania Bilal Meghabghab. Libraries Unlimited. (800) 237-6124.

Table 2.3 Data Gathering Scheme for the Information Service Function

Weekly_____   Monthly_____   Annually_____

Tasks	Number	Time	Frequency	Accuracy
Patrons with library cards				
Patrons who use the media center/library				
Patrons who use the card catalog				
Patrons who request assistance with the card catalog				
Staff assist patrons with the card catalog				
Bibliography compilation or other activity using the card catalog (by staff)				
Patrons' use of the subject card catalog				
Patrons' use of the title card catalog				
Patrons' use of the author card catalog				
Staff use of the card catalog				
Other tasks:				
Total/Average				

From *Automating Media Centers and Small Libraries.* © 1997. Dania Bilal Meghabghab. Libraries Unlimited. (800) 237-6124.

Table 2.4 Data Gathering Scheme for the Acquisitions Function

Weekly_____   Monthly_____   Annually_____

Tasks	Number	Time	Frequency	Accuracy
Item purchases				
Item verification				
Purchase order preparation				
Fund encumbrance				
Budget administration				
Item received				
Item returned				
Item claimed				
Acquisitions reports generated				
Record keeping				
Other tasks:				
Total/Average				

Table 2.5 Data Gathering Scheme for the Serials Function

Weekly_____   Monthly_____   Annually_____

Tasks	Number	Time	Frequency	Accuracy
Serials subscription				
Serials checked in				
Serials routed				
Serials claimed				
Serials reports generated				
Record keeping				
Other tasks:				
Total/Average				

If you find the circulation function is the most tedious, demanding, and repetitive, for example, and that there is a need to increase its effectiveness, accuracy, and efficiency, then that function is a prime candidate for automation. Similarly, if a user survey indicates that the greatest demand or need is to assist users in finding information and to improve access to the collection, then public access is the highest priority. It is worth noting that the public access function, which is supported by OPAC in an automated environment, cannot be implemented without the cataloging function; this gives both OPAC and cataloging functions equal priority. For information about how to conduct a use study, refer to the resources at the end of this chapter.

Data collection and analysis are useful, even when funds are available to automate all functions and, therefore, prioritization is not needed. In this case, the data provide a framework for establishing essential specifications that meet the media center's or library's needs and requirements. The data may indicate, for example, that patrons using the card catalog have difficulty retrieving information by subject. In this case, the subject and keyword search capabilities of the automated systems under consideration must be evaluated as they relate to the users' needs.

■ Funding

Automating for the purpose of saving money doesn't work. Automation improves media center or library services; enhances access to the collection; and increases productivity, accuracy, and efficiency in performing tasks. Because automation saves time in executing tasks and rendering service, it may allow staff more time to help users and to create new services. Therefore, during the initial stages of the planning process, the focus should be on how to proceed with automation and what needs to be accomplished rather than how much it costs (Wright 1995). After the benefits of automation are revealed and a justification for automation is established, the availability of monies or sources of funding can be investigated.

In seeking monies to fund an automation project, one does not to seek funding for automating all functions at once. As mentioned earlier, prioritizing functions allows one to phase in automation, thus allowing for budget constraints. (For more information about budgeting for automation, refer to the resources listed at the end of this chapter.)

□ Sources of Funding

Automation may be state funded or supported by external sources, such as computer companies, local businesses, Friends of the Library groups, community groups, and philanthropic organizations and foundations (Anderson 1996; Hayes and Brown 1992; Thompson 1992).

Funding for the automation project should be assessed during the preparation process to determine what funds will be available for present and future support. If funds are not available to acquire all modules in an automated system, for example, then consider phasing in the project by acquiring one module at a time, based on your priorities for automation. If funds are available, a decision may need to be made as to whether to hire an automation consultant to assist with the project. If you feel comfortable about gathering information and learning about the automation process, you may not need a consultant. Even when a consultant is hired, the final decision about selecting an automated system should lie with the automation committee, not the consultant.

☐ Cost Estimates

Budgeting for the automation project requires a cost estimate for the overall project, including ongoing expenses. The cost estimate should include software, hardware, utilities, supplies, personnel, and ongoing expenses.

The cost estimate for software includes the automation software and other software that supports the operation of the automated system, such as software for barcode or label production, software for in-house retrospective conversion, or a Web browser to provide access to OPAC on the World Wide Web.

Hardware may include computer stations, a host system or file server, printers, scanners, inventory devices, an uninterruptable power supply (UPS) for the file server, modems, and the hardware needed to create a local area network (LAN). The cost of the LAN will depend on the network topology (i.e., the cabling system) and network architecture (i.e., Token Ring, Ethernet, FDDI) selected. For a more detailed discussion of LANs and the hardware required for them, see chapter 7.

Utilities include retrospective conversion, Internet access, site licenses for multi-user access, update of existing wiring, installation of additional telephone lines, remodeling the facilities, and furniture.

Supplies pertain to barcode labels for both materials and patrons, barcode protectors, library cards, due date cards, overdue notices, paper for printers, and the like. Supplies are also considered ongoing expenses.

Personnel costs pertains to hiring a consultant, new staff, and certified personnel for cable installation or other tasks as needed. Personnel costs also cover staff training for attending automation workshops and training in the use of the automation software after the system is implemented.

Ongoing expenses include software updates, technical support, software and hardware maintenance, telecommunications charges, and supplies. The cost of these project components can be found in product catalogs and through communications with vendors.

■ Summary

Preparing for automation is an essential activity in the automation process. It involves knowledge acquisition, needs assessment, and budgeting. Needs assessment is conducted to examine and evaluate the media center's or library's goals and objectives, procedures, and functions and to collect data about each function for the purpose of justifying and prioritizing its automation. Workflow diagrams provide a clear understanding of the tasks involved in each function. Needs assessment is also performed to determine user and staff needs. Knowledge acquisition of the automation process and staff involvement are vital for the success of any automation project.

Above all, one must remember that automation does not save money. It is cost-effective, it increases productivity and efficiency, and it enhances access to the media center's or library's collection. The focus during planning should be on these benefits and on how to proceed with automation rather than how much it costs.

■ References

Anderson, Mary Alice. 1996. Technology dollars from pennies saved. *Book Report* 14 (January/February): 13, 15.

Barry, Jeff, Jose-Marie Griffiths, and Wang Peiling. 1996. Jockeying for supremacy in a networked world: Automated system marketplace 1996. *Library Journal* 121 (April): 40–51.

Chen, Shu-Hsien. 1991. A study of online catalog searching behavior of high school students. Ed.D. diss., University of Georgia.

Cibbarelli, Pamela, ed. 1996. *Directory of library automation software, systems, and services.* Medford, NJ: Information Today.

Cohn, John M., Ann L. Kelsey, and Keith M. Fiels. 1992. *Planning for automation.* New York: Neil-Schuman.

Cortez, Edwin M., and Tom Smorch. 1993. *Planning second generation automated systems.* Westport, CT: Greenwood Press.

Edmonds, Leslie, Paula Moore, and Kathleen M. Balcom. 1990. The effectiveness of an online catalog. *School Library Journal* 36 (October): 28–32.

Freeman, Gretchen L., and Russell T. Clement. 1989. Critical issues in library automation and staff training. *The Electronic Library* 7 (April): 76–82.

Havelock, Ronald G., and Steve Zlotolow. 1995. *The change agent's guide.* 2d ed. Englewood Cliffs, NJ: Educational Technology Publications.

Hayes, Sherman, and Donald Brown. 1992. Creative budgeting and funding for automation: Getting the goods! *Wilson Library Bulletin* 66 (April): 42–45.

Hirsh, Sandra G., and Christine Borgman L. 1995. Comparing children's use of browsing and keyword searching on the science library catalog. *Proceedings of the American Society for Information Science,* 19–26.

Jacobson, Francis F. 1991. Information retrieval systems and youth: A review of recent literature. *Journal of Youth Services in Libraries* 5 (Fall): 109–13.

Kemp, Jan. 1995. Reevaluating support staff positions. *Library Administration and Management* 9 (Winter): 37–43.

Kilgour, Frederick G. 1991. Online access will reduce author/title catalog search failure. *Online Review* 15 (October): 307–14.

Krol, Carol. 1995. Updating the school library. *Media & Methods* 32 (January/February): 8, 15.

Kuhlthau, Carol C. 1991. Inside the search process: Information seeking from the user's perspective. *Journal of the American Society for Information Science* 42 (June): 361–71.

Lighthall, Lynne. 1989. A planning and implementation guide for automating school libraries: Selecting a system. *School Libraries in Canada* 8 (Winter): 27–36.

Muir, Scott P. 1991. Automation of a small corporate library. *Library Software Review* 10 (September/October): 316–319.

Mullen, Al, and Sara Laughlin. 1996. Preparing for automation. INCOLSA home page. Copyright 1996. http://www.palni.edu/~al/workshop1/automate.htm. (Accessed February 21, 1997.)

Oberg, Larry R. 1995. Library support staff in an age of change: Utilization, role definition and status. ERIC Document ED 382197.

Sherouse, Vicki M. 1995. Automate your library in two years under $4,000. *Technology Connection* 2 (October): 18–20.

Sliveke, Krystal K. 1991. Library automation: Survey of chemical (sci-tech) libraries within for-profit corporations in Ohio. Master's thesis, Kent State University.

Solomon, Paul. 1994. Children, technology, and instruction: A case study of elementary school children using an Online Public Access Catalog (OPAC). *School Library Media Quarterly* 23 (Fall): 43–51.

Thompson, Ronelle K. H. 1992. Funding for library automation. ERIC Document ED 353987.

Whitney, Gretchen, and Stuart Glogoff. 1994. Automation for the nineties: A review article. *Library Quarterly* 64 (July): 319–31.

Wildemuth, Barbara M., and Ann L. O'Neill. 1995. The "known" in known-item searches: Empirical support for user-centered design. *College & Research Libraries* 56 (May): 265–81.

Winstead, Elizabeth B. 1994. Staff reactions to automation. *Computers in Libraries* 14 (April): 18–21.

Wright, Kieth C. 1995. Computer-related technologies in library operations. Brookfield, VT: Gower.

Activity: Data Gathering and Analysis

Objective 1: To analyze various workflow patterns and diagram them.

Description: 1. Collect information about the procedures and workflow patterns of various functions and tasks performed in a nonautomated media center or small library. You may interview a media specialist or information professional to determine the patterns.

2. Prepare a workflow diagram for each task performed for each function. Create a separate workflow diagram for each task in a function, with identifiable starting and stopping points. Represent the procedures of each task from start to finish. Enumerate each procedure on the diagram.

3. Briefly describe each procedure illustrated in the diagram on a separate sheet.

Objective 2: To gather data about the functions of a media center or a small library; this data could be used to build arguments for automation and to prioritize the functions to be automated.

Description: 1. Select a nonautomated media center or a small library and describe:

its mission and goals,

the number of clients it serves,

existing user services,

collection size, and

new services to be implemented.

2. Gather data about the functions of the media center or small library using the scheme provided in tables 2.1–2.5.

3. Examine the workflow diagrams developed for the first part of this activity. Link the collected data to the respective tasks.

4. Determine the tasks that are most repetitive, tedious, and labor-intensive.

5. Determine the tasks that may involve inaccuracy, inefficiency, and low productivity.

6. Select functions for automation and justify your decision. Prioritize the functions and, again, justify your decision. If all functions are of equal priority, provide strong justification for your decision.

3 Hardware Configurations for Automation Software

■ Automated systems software must be capable of performing simple and sophisticated tasks and must comply with the latest bibliographic standards. In this, not all systems are created equal. Capabilities vary according to platform (Macintosh or IBM-PC compatible), operating system (e.g., Macintosh, MS-DOS, Windows, Windows NT, UNIX), and the kind of computer (i.e., microcomputer, minicomputer, and mainframe) used. Capabilities refer to the functions or tasks an automated system can perform, the size of collection it can accommodate, the number and size of patron records it can store, and its interface with other systems or tools (e.g., OCLC, Georgia Online Database, the Internet). To select the best system for a specific automation project, one must match the needs, requirements, and financial resources of the media center or library to the capabilities and costs of the various hardware and software.

During the past five years, advances in technology have blurred the differences between various types of computer systems. Microcomputers with operating systems such as Windows NT, Windows 95, and IBM Operating System/2 Warp (OS/2 Warp) have achieved processing power comparable to mainframes and miniframes (Van Name and Catchings 1995). In addition, the past five years have seen rapid changes in software, including operating systems. The increased power of microcomputers makes it possible for media centers and small libraries to take advantage of automated systems that were before only available to institutions with large, expensive computer systems. This chapter describes the characteristics, advantages, and disadvantages of various hardware configurations for automation using microcomputers.

Automation using mainframes and miniframes is beyond the scope of this book; however many of the topics discussed here in relation to microcomputers will apply equally well, or with some adaptation, to media centers and small libraries that are networked to mainframes.

■ Classes of Computers

From the smallest to the largest, computers used for automation fall into three classes: microcomputers, minicomputers, and mainframes. This section focuses on microcomputers. For more information about types of computers and their capabilities, as well as their advantages and disadvantages for automation, see "The Decision(s) to Automate the Card Catalog," by Robert Skapura (1990).

□ Microcomputers

Microcomputers are also known as personal, desktop, or portable computers. They are used in offices, homes, schools, laboratories, and other facilities. They can be used to support stand-alone, or independent, operations and to create a local area network (LAN) or a wide area network (WAN). The cost of a microcomputer ranges from $2,000 to more than $5,000, depending on the amount of random access memory (RAM), hard disk storage capacity, type and number of microprocessors, clock speed, and peripherals.

Most media centers and small libraries will use a microcomputer-based automation system. This book assumes a basic knowledge of microcomputers, but readers who require more information about them may refer to Marcel Dekker's *Encyclopedia of Microcomputers* (1996) or *Computers Simplified* by Ruth Maran (1996).

□ Automation Software for Various Classes of Computers

Automation software may operate on mainframes, miniframes, or microcomputers. Some software is written specifically for a certain type of computer (i.e., a mainframe); other software is compatible with more than one type of computer (i.e., it may run on both mainframes and microcomputers). Generally speaking, the automation software for miniframes and mainframes is designed to handle the high volume of operations generated in medium-sized and larger academic, special, and public libraries. Most automated systems designed for use in media centers and small libraries are microcomputer-based. Recently, many medium-sized libraries have started to shift to microcomputer-based systems.

An example of a microcomputer-based automation system is Unison, from Follett Software Company, which runs on Windows NT, MS-DOS, and Macintosh operating systems. An example of a miniframe-based automated system is Virginia Tech Library System (VTLS), which operates on UNIX and Hewlett-Packard proprietary operating system MPE/IX.

■ Options for Hardware Configurations Using Microcomputers

Three hardware configurations are most often used for automated systems in media centers and small libraries: microcomputer stand-alone, microcomputer stand-alone with CD-ROM, and networked microcomputers with a file server.

□ Microcomputer Stand-Alone

This configuration consists of one or more microcomputer stand-alone stations that function independently. The automation software is installed on each computer's hard disk, so that each computer holds everything it needs to perform automated functions. This configuration is found most often in a media center or library with a small collection, small number of users, or limited financial resources. Libraries that start automation with one module may choose this hardware configuration. It's important to note that a stand-alone hardware configuration is different from a stand-alone software system described in chapter 2. Integrated software may be used with the stand-alone hardware configuration.

There are distinct advantages to the stand-alone configuration. One advantage is financial: Libraries that cannot afford a LAN may choose a stand-alone configuration. Other advantages pertain to operation and services: Because each computer operates independently, the malfunction of one computer will not affect the operation of others. Because the database resides on the hard drive of the computer(s) in the library, the database can be updated as frequently as the media specialist or information professional likes, and updates can be performed online. Remote dial-up access is possible if each station is equipped with a modem.

However, the stand-alone configuration has a few disadvantages. A site license is required for multi-user access; this adds to the cost of the software. Installing the original software and updating it must be done on each computer station. The more stations, the more time-consuming it is to install and update the software. Troubleshooting software problems is time-consuming, especially when more than one or two computer stations malfunction at the same time, because each station may have a different problem.

☐ Microcomputer Stand-Alone with CD-ROM

This configuration is similar to the microcomputer stand-alone configuration, except that the automation software operates from one or more CD-ROMs rather than each computer's hard disk. To make this work, each computer station is equipped with a CD-ROM player. This configuration is associated with the software rather than the hardware, meaning that the software is only available on CD-ROM.

This configuration has one advantage of the stand-alone configuration, that is, the malfunction of one stand-alone computer will not affect the operation of the others, because each computer works independently. Other advantages relate to cost: Because CD-ROMs can hold large amounts of data, the automation software and enhancements fit on one disk. This reduces the cost of updates.

But this configuration has disadvantages as well. Prompt access to new items that are added to the collection is hampered, because updating the collection database can only be done by creating a new master CD-ROM of MARC records. This can be expensive. The Library Corporation, owner of Bibliofile automation software, charges $150 for each CD-ROM created. An annual subscription for quarterly updates costs $550 (Sweeney 1996). Obviously, if there is more than one stand-alone computer with a CD-ROM, the cost of updates must be multiplied by the number of computer stations requiring the updated disk. One option for lowering the cost of updates is to share the cost of updating CD-ROMs among media centers or libraries in a cooperative venture, such as a union catalog. This makes frequent (e.g., monthly) database updates affordable.

If timely access to the collection and an interface or integration among various modules are priorities for the media center or library, this configuration is *not* recommended. Special and public libraries, because of the kinds of clients they serve, may not wish to consider this configuration.

☐ Networked Microcomputers with File Server

In this configuration, a microcomputer station, called a file server, is dedicated to (i.e., used only for) storing data and sharing resources among several remote stations or computers in a networked environment. A file server may have 1 gigabyte (GB) RAM, a 4GB hard drive, 200 megahertz (MHz) clock speed, and a 586 microprocessor or higher. Several microcomputers are connected to the file server by cables to create a local area network (LAN) or a wide area network (WAN). The automation software is installed and updated on the file server(s). (A LAN or WAN requires more than one file server to accommodate the various operations performed in the institution.) This configuration is recommended for any media center or small library that can afford to create a LAN or WAN and also the cost of the software and network maintenance.

One of the greatest advantages of a networked system is that updates to the database can be made online, providing users speedy access to items added to the collection. Other advantages are:

- As with a stand-alone configuration, users who are equipped with a computer and a modem can dial into OPAC from remote locations. The advantage in the LAN environment is the configuration of modems in the media center or library. In a LAN environment, one modem installed on the file server is all that is needed to provide dial-up access for users. In contrast, with stand-alone configurations, one modem is needed for each computer station, or one of the stations must be dedicated to dial-up callers. In a LAN environment, because the file server is the dedicated station, other computer stations are freed for user access.

- A file server with a modem makes it possible for vendors to diagnose and troubleshoot software problems online (that is, at the file server), thus providing quick solutions to problems. In a stand-alone configuration, diagnosing problems must be done separately for each malfunctioning computer station. With the file server configuration, diagnoses is done on the file server, not on each individual computer station.

Although the advantages of a file server configuration are many, there are several disadvantages. Greatest of these is that the malfunction of a file server affects all networked stations. Downtime hampers access to the collection and may cause frustration on the part of users and staff. It also detracts from the efficiency that is supposed to be achieved through automation. Other disadvantages of the file server configuration include:

- The speed and quality of data transmission in a networked environment depends on the type of cable used (e.g., coaxial, twisted pair, fiber) and the network architecture (e.g., Ethernet, Token Ring, Fiber Distributed Data Interface [FDDI]). The use of a low-end cable, for example, will slow the network's performance, but a high-end cable is more costly.

- Remote access to the automated system may be delayed or denied when telephone lines are occupied, which may distress users. This not only frustrates users, it interferes with the efficiency that automation is supposed to introduce.

- Generally, the hardware and software needed for networked systems are more costly than those needed for the stand-alone configuration. Networking computer stations is very costly, because it requires a file server, a licensing fee, and a networking card for each station; these costs may amount to more than $15,000. The cost of a file server ranges from $5,000 to $200,000, depending on the hard disk storage capacity, RAM, the type and number of microprocessors, clock speed, and the number of clients (computer stations) or resources (operations) serviced.

- Maintenance and troubleshooting require knowledge of and skills in computer networking. Media specialists and information professionals who lack this knowledge must rely on experienced personnel—either experienced staff or outside consultants. One problem with using staff in this capacity is that other demands on the staff person's time may take precedence over the needs of the media center or library. Of course, the problem with using outside experts is cost.

■ Summary

Computer systems used for automation fall into three main categories: microcomputers, miniframes, and mainframes. Microcomputers are the systems typically used in media centers and small libraries. Powerful microcomputers have similar power to miniframes and mainframes.

There are three configuration options for hardware: microcomputer stand-alone, microcomputer stand-alone with CD-ROM, and microcomputer with file server. Each configuration has advantages and disadvantages.

Generally speaking, a stand-alone configuration may be the best choice for a media center or library with three to five computer stations, where networking is unaffordable. The stand-alone configuration with CD-ROM hampers timely access to the collection and does not provide users with the benefits of integrated automated systems (e.g., allowing users to determine the circulation status of items found in OPAC) because the database supporting each function (e.g., circulation, cataloging, acquisitions, serials) is stored on a separate CD-ROM. The preferred configuration in any networked environment, especially a local area network, is the file server.

■ References

Encyclopedia of microcomputers. 1996. New York: Marcel Dekker.

Maran, Ruth. 1996. *Computers simplified.* San Mateo, CA: IDG Books.

Meghabghab, Dania Bilal. 1994. Purchasing a microcomputer-based automated system for schools and public libraries: Points to consider and pitfalls to avoid. *Proceedings of the Ninth Integrated Online Library Systems Meeting,* New York, May, pp. 139–46.

O'Leary, Timothy J., and Linda I. O'Leary. 1995. *Computing essentials.* New York: McGraw-Hill.

Skapura, Robert. 1990. The decision(s) to automate the card catalog. *California Media and Library Educators Association Journal* 14 (Fall): 9–12.

Sweeney, Jason. 1996. Telephone conversation with the author. Sweeney is a sales representative at The Library Corporation, producers of Bibliofile automation software.

Van Name, Mark L., and Bill Catchings. 1995. Your high-maintenance PC. Copyright 1996. http://www.zdnet.com. (Accessed April 3, 1996.)

Activity: Hardware Configurations

Objective: To examine the hardware configuration of an automated system used in a media center or small library.

Description: 1.   Select a media center or a small library that has an automated system. Meet with either the media specialist or information professional, technology coordinator or specialist, or other qualified personnel. Gather information about the hardware configuration, including the

- type of configuration used (e.g., stand-alone, CD-ROM, file server),

- number of existing computer stations,

- type of platform used (i.e., Macintosh or PC),

- type of operating system used (e.g., DOS, Windows, etc.),

- name of automation software and the modules implemented,

- cost of the automation software,

- cost of the hardware configuration, and

- reasons for selecting the existing configuration.

2.   Write a report describing the mission of the media center or small library, the number of patrons it serves, and the size of its collection. Also describe the strengths and weaknesses of the existing configuration from the media specialist's, information professional's or other qualified personnel's perspective, and your own perspective about the configuration's strengths and weaknesses. Describe the configuration you would choose or the modifications you would make to the existing configuration to best meet the media center's or library's mission and serve its patrons. Justify your answer.

4 System Selection

The rapid advancement of computer technology has had a marked impact on the development of automation software. An automated system is no longer a replica of the card catalog; instead, it offers colossal features the card catalog could never provide. As additional advances are made, future automated systems will offer even more and better features. For this reason, automation software must be supported by a company that is committed to enhancing the software on a regular basis. Hence, knowledge of a company's history, stability, experience in automation, quality of service, responsiveness to users' needs, and present and future directions in developing the software are key criteria for selecting an automated system. This is, of course, in addition to the capabilities of the automation software itself.

This chapter covers essential steps in selecting an integrated microcomputer-based automated system and reveals pitfalls to avoid during the selection process.

■ The Selection Process

The first step in selecting a microcomputer-based automated system is re-examination of the needs assessment conducted during the preparation process to recollect your priority needs, staff needs, user information needs, and budget.

☐ Select Six Packages

The knowledge about the automation process that you acquired during the preparation process, and your review of the literature, should assist you in identifying the automated software to consider. Select six software packages suitable for your media center or library to review more thoroughly. Consult the latest issues of *Library Technology Reports* containing reviews of the software packages under consideration. Take notes about the strengths and weaknesses of each module, along with the rating of the overall system. The latter is provided on a scale ranging from 1 to 10. Generally speaking, to be considered, the rating of a software package should not fall below 9 on the 10-point scale. Note that system selection should not be based on reviews only; your testing and evaluation of the packages to determine their suitability for your needs and requirements is also important.

Next, preview each package yourself. Request a demonstration diskette from each vendor, but be aware that the demonstrations on such diskettes may be incomplete or not interactive. For more complete, interactive demonstrations, visit libraries that have recently implemented each system you are considering. This will allow you to experiment with many applications online and also to see how well the software operates in real situations.

Invite a sales representative from each of the six software companies to demonstrate the software in-house. If you invited company representatives to discuss their software during the preparation process, invite them again, because by this time you have gained more knowledge about automation and are better prepared to ask more specific and in-depth questions. Prepare a list of questions to ask each representative; use the notes from your reading and software previews to help you develop your questions. Demonstrations provided by representatives usually reflect the latest software enhancements, thus giving you up-to-date information that has not yet appeared in the literature.

☐ Narrow Your Choices

Compile and examine all your notes from initial knowledge acquisition, later readings, previews, and demonstrations to screen the six software choices now before you. Remember to ask all members of the automation committee for their input. Based on your notes and discussion of the automation committee, narrow your choice to three software packages that best meet your needs and requirements. In narrowing your choices, consider the following criteria:

> the capability to integrate multiple modules;
>
> presence of all modules needed;
>
> presence of essential features in each module;
>
> strengths of each module;
>
> overall software capabilities (e.g., for multi-user access, Internet access, networking, expandability);

compliance with the latest bibliographic standards (i.e., U.S. MARC and U.S. MARC/MicroLIF) and the information retrieval standard Z39.50;

software ratings;

the software vendor's plans for providing new applications;

the software vendor's plans for enhancing existing applications;

frequency of software updates;

quality of service provided by the software company (e.g., technical support, turnaround time for assistance) and the hours that service is available;

software documentation and its organization;

type and cost of training provided; and

cost of the software, software updates, and annual support.

To facilitate the preliminary screening process, you may develop a list of specifications based on these criteria and the general specifications provided in the sample request for proposal, or RFP. (RFPs are discussed later in this chapter.)

□ Develop a Request for Proposal (RFP)

After you have narrowed your list of software choices to three packages, subject these three packages to detailed comparison and evaluation. To do this, develop an RFP based on the needs assessment, your notes, checklists or sample RFPs supplied by software companies, RFPs developed by media centers and libraries that have implemented automation, RFPs included in the literature (like the one in this chapter), and consultation with colleagues.

Why develop an RFP? An RFP provides means for comparing and evaluating various systems and for selecting a system that best suits your needs. Developing an RFP is one of the most important steps in procuring an automated system. "Even when an RFP is not required, it is a useful part of the procurement process because it forces you to determine your automation needs" (Day, Flanders, and Zuck 1994). An RFP may be more than a guide for comparison, however; it may result in a binding agreement between a media center or library and a vendor, which stipulates the specifications an automated system must meet.

Many software vendors supply customers with their own sample RFPs or checklists. Vendors maintain that lengthy RFPs are unnecessary when automation software is supported by well-established companies (Barry, Griffiths, and Lundeen 1995). In fact, companies' RFPs, although useful, contain specifications that are tailored to their own systems. Regardless of how well a vendor's RFP is developed, it is recommended that you develop your own.

■ Preparing the Request for Proposal (RFP)

Preparing an RFP requires knowledge of an automated system's functional specifications so that one is able to respond to a vendor's questions and explain the specifications described. Although RFPs may vary in format, certain things are essential. These are consistency of organization, use of appropriate verbs, specificity of the specifications, and a good writing style. A sample RFP appears on pages 51–83. Following are suggestions for writing an RFP:

- Organize the RFP into sections, including separate sections devoted to each module.

- Use the word *must* to indicate the essential specifications and the word *should* to indicate desirable or preferred specifications. *Essential specifications* are those you cannot do without; *desirable* or *preferred specifications* are nice to have but you can do without them.

- List the tasks the system should perform, rather than how it should do them.

- Include specifications for all modules desired in a system.

- Describe specifications the system must incorporate at present and in the near future.

- Define all of the codes, symbols, descriptors, and scales you use, and give vendors instructions about how to apply them.

- Use the following verbs: *allow, display, design, perform, provide, detect, initiate, generate, search, calculate, maintain, can, capable of, prompt,* and the like, as applicable.

- When the vendor is asked to rate the software's ability to meet specifications using a scale (e.g., 1–5 or 1–10), ask the vendor to explain any below-average ratings.

- Allow sufficient space at the end of each section for the vendor's response or comments.

- Request a copy of the company's latest audited financial statement. Also request the names of media centers or libraries (especially those in your state) that have implemented the software. Ask for the names of key personnel and a market survey or studies about the system. This information is essential for evaluating the company's stability and the qualifications of its key personnel, especially those in the technical support and processing units.

- Allow vendors four to six weeks to respond to the RFP.

☐ Organizing the RFP

The first page of the RFP includes a cover sheet with the title of the RFP, the name of the person to whom it is submitted, the company name and address, the name and address of the contact person in the media center or library, and the submission date.

The second page is a table of contents. The following pages may include six main sections in the following order:

- Instructions to the vendor
- Introduction to the media center or library
- Software specifications (both essential and preferred)
- Hardware specifications
- Request for price quotation
- Notice of intent to respond

The following sections briefly describe each part of the RFP.

Instructions to the Vendor

This section explains the organization of the RFP. It defines the descriptors (e.g., essential and preferred), rating system or scale (e.g., 1–5 or 1–10), or codes (e.g., A = Available, N = Not available, U = Under development, F = Future development) used.

Introduction to the Media Center or Library

This section provides brief background information about the media center or library, its goals and objectives, and how these goals and objectives relate to automation. Reports based on the data gathered during the planning process may be included.

Software Specifications

This section lists the essential and preferred specifications for each module of the automated system. This is the heart of the RFP. For an example of software specifications, see figures 4.1–4.8, pages 52–80.

Hardware Specifications

This section provides specifications for the essential hardware, that is, hardware that is required to support the automation system. In some cases, one vendor provides both the hardware and the software needed for the automated system. In other cases, the software vendor does not supply the needed hardware. If this is the case for any of the software packages you are considering, then you must develop a separate RFP for the needed hardware.

Hardware includes a file server or other computer system, printer(s), client computer stations, barcode scanner(s), and other hardware or equipment needed to support the operation of the system. (The required hardware depends on what configuration you are planning to use for your automated system. See chapter 3 for a discussion of three common configurations.)

Specifications for a file server are supplied in figure 4.9, page 81. Additional specifications should be developed for other pieces of hardware. You can find examples of hardware specifications in Day, Flanders and Zuck (1994).

Note: Different software packages have different hardware requirements (e.g., some packages run only in networked environments, some run only on certain platforms, some require CD-ROM readers). Software vendors usually provide specifications for the hardware required to run their packages. These specifications must be examined before developing the RFP for hardware. Look for them in the vendors' product catalogs.

Request for Price Quotation

This section provides a form for the vendor to complete. The form, developed by the RFP writer, may include a description of each item or feature required (i.e., system modules, multi-user access, record conversion, barcodes, barcode scanners). The vendor is asked to provide the list price of each item, the applicable discounted price, the cost of a maintenance contract, the cost of updates and enhancements, and the cost of any other items or features that are important to the operation of the system. It is best to request a 30-day price guarantee (fixed price) for the listed items.

Notice of Intent to Respond

The notice of intent to respond is a form included with the RFP. The vendor fills out and returns the form to let the media specialist or information professional know that a response to the submitted RFP is forthcoming. Allow four to six weeks for the vendor to respond.

☐ Review the RFP and Send It to Vendors

After the RFP is written, have members of the automation committee plus one or two outside experts in automation (e.g., professor of automation at a nearby college or university) or colleagues experienced in automation review it and provide you with feedback. Prepare a final draft of the RFP, incorporating the reviewers' feedback.

Duplicate and mail the RFP to each of the three software companies under consideration.

☐ Evaluate Responses to the RFP and Choose One Package

Examine each company's response to the RFP to determine the software's strengths and weaknesses. Then compare and evaluate the RFPs for a final screening. Select the software package that best meets your essential specifications. If two or three packages are comparable or equal in this respect (which is unlikely), then the determining factors are the quality of service provided by the vendor, the cost of the software, and the annual cost of technical support.

☐ Contract to Purchase the Software

After selecting one of the software packages, contact the vendor to draft a contract to purchase the software. The contract with the vendor must include

> a schedule for software delivery, installation, testing, and implementation;
>
> a schedule for training personnel to use the software;
>
> the vendor's promise to deliver a software package that meets the specifications stipulated in the RFP;
>
> the vendor's comments or explanations about certain specifications, ratings of features, and plans for providing enhancements and updates; and
>
> a payment plan. If you are not financing the purchase, consider paying for it in three installments: one-third upon signing the contract, one-third upon successful installation and performance testing, and a final payment upon successful performance over time (Mullen 1996).

Have your media center's or library's attorney review the contract before you sign it.

■ Pitfalls to Avoid

Making mistakes during the selection process is inevitable, especially when a decision is made to automate without provision of adequate time and staff training. Careful preparation, as outlined in chapter 2, will help you avoid common pitfalls. Nevertheless, sometimes unexpected events—even windfalls—can take media specialists and librarians by surprise. This was the case in the state of Georgia in 1994, when the governor decided to use revenues from lottery funds to automate every media center in the state. Media specialists were unprepared and lacked knowledge of automation.

Following are some common traps that unwary media specialists or librarians may fall into. Good planning and awareness of the pitfalls will help you to avoid them.

★ = Discussed in class

- Assuming cost indicates suitability. The cost of a package does not always "guarantee a product appropriate for the specific application" of the media center or library (Bridge 1993). This means that you should not overemphasize cost in deciding which software package is best. Do not eliminate software packages that are slightly more expensive than your budget allows. The extra cost may be worth it. "The more expensive packages offer more complete training, better support, and a wider range of capabilities" (Bridge 1993).

- Being taken in by the charm or the educational background or experience of the sales representative. The sales representative's job is to impress you in order to sell the product. Focus on the product, not the representative.

- Purchasing a system based solely on the software preview, a colleague's recommendation, or cost. Thoroughly test and evaluate the software packages. Remember to involve staff in this process.

- Selecting a system without developing your own RFP. No "canned" RFP can do justice to the unique requirements of your media center or library. Although time-consuming, creating a customized RFP is essential to ensure that the automation system will meet the unique needs of your media center or library. If necessary, you must convince staff and administration (and yourself) of the need for a customized RFP.

- Choosing a system before evaluating and comparing vendors' responses to the RFP. Allow adequate time to examine vendors' responses to your RFP. Eliminate all software packages that do not meet 90 percent of your needs and requirements.

■ Evaluating the RFP Before Sending It Out

Do your homework before making a decision. Research existing systems, find reviews, consult with colleagues, test the software yourself, have users as well as staff test the software and give your their feedback, and compare systems' specifications to the needs and requirements of the media center or library.

■ Summary

Selecting an automated system is a time-consuming task that takes a long-term commitment of financial and personnel resources. The selection decision should be based on needs assessment, research, evaluation, and comparison of existing systems. Although time-consuming, developing an RFP is highly recommended, even when systems under consideration are supported by well-known and reputable automation companies. An RFP is the best means of articulating the specifications an automated system must and should meet; it allows comparison among various systems and provides justification for selecting a particular system.

Media specialists and information professionals must be involved not only in the selection process, but also in the decision about system procurement, because they are the most knowledgeable personnel about the collection, users' needs and information-seeking behavior, and administrative conditions of their workplace.

■ References

Barry, Jeff, Jose-Marie Griffiths, and Gerald W. Lundeen. 1995. The changing face of automation. *Library Journal* 120 (April): 44–54.

Bender, Eric, and William L. Rinko-Gay. 1996. Top 3 workgroup servers. Available: http://www.pcworld.com. (Accessed June 26, 1996.)

Boss, Richard W. 1990. The procurement of library automated systems. *Library Technology Reports* 26 (Spring): 629–749.

Bridge, Frank R. 1993. Automated system marketplace 1993. *Library Journal* 118 (April): 50–55.

Cohn, John M., Ann L. Kelsey, and Keith M. Fields. 1992. *Planning for automation*. New York: Neal-Schuman.

Day, Teresa Thurman, Bruce Flanders, and Gregory Zuck, eds. 1994. Automation for school libraries: How to do it from those who have done it. Chicago: American Library Association.

Lighthall, Lynne. 1989. A planning and implementation guide for automating school libraries: Selecting a system. *School Libraries in Canada* 8 (Winter): 27–36.

Maddan, Mary, and Ed Tittel. 1996. Network servers: reliably yours. Available: http://www.pcworld.com. (Accessed June 26, 1996.)

Meghabghab, Dania Bilal. 1994. Purchasing a microcomputer-based automated system for school and public libraries: Points to consider and pitfalls to avoid. *Proceedings of the Ninth Integrated Online Library Systems Meeting*, New York, May, pp. 139–46.

Mullen, Al. 1996. Planning for automation. INCOLSA home page. Copyright 1996. http://www.palni.edu/~al/autoworkshop1/automate.htm. (Accessed February 21, 1997.)

Activity: Cost Analysis

Objective 1:   To select specific software and conduct a cost analysis.

Description: 1.   Select an integrated automated system for which you would like to conduct a cost analysis. Perform the following activities:

Provide the quantity, brief description, and cost of each module, as applicable.

Contact the software vendor for information about the cost of the software and other supporting products, if supplied (e.g., barcode scanner). Many software vendors supply associated hardware and supplies, such as barcode scanners and barcode labels.

Determine the cost of technical support, training, and updates.

Calculate the total cost.

Objective 2:   To select hardware compatible with the software and perform a cost analysis.

Description: 1.   Identify the hardware needed to support the operation of the automation software chosen in Objective One. Perform the following activities:

Provide the quantity, item description, and item cost for the following: a file server, printer(s), lookup stations, inventory device(s), barcode scanner(s), uninterruptible power supply unit (for the file server), networking operating system, networking cards, and maintenance.

Calculate the cost of the hardware.

Calculate the total cost of software and hardware.

2. Provide the names, addresses, and telephone numbers of the vendors contacted for the software and hardware. List the catalogs and other materials consulted for this cost analysis on a separate sheet.

3. Describe any problems or difficulties you encountered in collecting the information. Was this activity valuable?

4. State the amount of time it took you to gather the information and to complete this activity.

Sample Request for Proposal

Figures 4.1–4.9 list the minimum essential specifications for an MS-DOS integrated microcomputer-based automated system that supports cataloging, authority control, OPAC, circulation, acquisitions, and serials. Specifications for hardware are provided for the file server only. (Specifications for other hardware components can be found in Day, Flanders, and Zuck [1994].)

The specifications provided in these examples may be modified to meet the specific needs and requirements of individual media centers and libraries. Because only minimum essential specifications are listed in the examples, preferred specifications must be added. On the other hand, a number of the specifications considered essential in this RFP may be merely preferred specifications for a particular media center or library. Again, the specifications must be tailored to meet the needs and preferences of each media center or library.

The sample RFP applies a numbering system to identify each feature described, as well as a scale and a code for the vendor to use in responding. To fill out this type of RFP, the vendor writes the appropriate scale or code in the box next to the feature being described. At the end of each section of the specifications list, additional space is provided for vendor comments. Vendors are instructed to refer to features by their identifying numbers when discussing them.

The sample RFP offered in this chapter is based on the author's lengthy experience in automation, consultation with practitioners, examination and evaluation of well-developed RFPs, and sources in the literature.

Figure 4.1   General essential specifications.

Codes for Column 3:   A = Available   N = Not available   U = Under development
                       F = Future development

Scale for Column 4   1–5:   1 = Very poor   5 = Excellent

Note: The term *must* means essential.

Feature Number	The system must:	Code: A-N-U-F	Scale: 1–5
G-1	support OPAC, circulation, cataloging, acquisitions, serials, utilities, U.S. MARC, inventory, and authority control in one fully integrated system.		
G-2	allow modules in G-1 to interface and to work both independently of and concurrently with each other.		
G-3	support menu- and command-driven user interfaces to accommodate experienced and novice users.		
G-4	support MS-DOS compatible microcomputers with a 586 microprocessor and 133 MHz clock speed or higher.		
G-5	be networkable, compatible with Novell Netware to support a local area network (LAN).		
G-6	accommodate simultaneous multi-user access of 100 existing computer stations and simultaneous multi-user access of a minimum of 200 stations in the near future.		
G-7	support telecommunications for simultaneous, remote dial-up access for a minimum of 100 users.		
G-8	accommodate a patron database of 50,000 and support its future growth to a minimum of 150,000.		
G-9	accommodate an existing collection size of 150,000 titles and support its future growth to 300,000.		
G-10	be compatible with brief and full U.S. MARC and U.S. MARC/MicroLIF Protocol formats.		
G-11	allow import and export of U.S. MARC and U.S. MARC/MicroLIF Protocol records.		
G-12	store, display, read, input, and output information in brief and full U.S. MARC and/or U.S. MARC/MicroLIF Protocol formats.		
G-13	transfer downloaded U.S. MARC records into U.S. MARC/MicroLIF Protocol records.		
G-14	allow program data backup while users are on the system.		
G-15	support nonproprietary, industry-standard barcode labels of at least 14 digits, as well as optical scanning devices (e.g., light pens, wands, laser guns, etc.).		

Continued on next page

Figure 4.1 **General essential specifications (continued).**

Feature Number	The system must:	Cose: A-N-U-F	Scale: 1–5
G-16	support the collection inventory using a portable barcode reader/scanner/laser gun.		
G-17	contain a utilities or equivalent module for customizing system features, such as loan codes and patron types, and to fix problems.		
G-18	provide authority control for author, title, subject, and series based on the Library of Congress U.S. MARC format.		
G-19	maintain a context-sensitive help and/or a help index for all screens.		
G-20	contain a multilayered security feature with passwords that allows staff to change passwords.		
G-21	allow data backup and restoration of database files in case of hardware and/or software failure.		
G-22	alert for backup before exiting.		
G-23	prevent unauthorized access of the software.		
G-24	allow deletion of files and/or records.		
G-25	alert for deletion of files and/or records.		
G-26	confirm deletion of files and/or records.		

G-27	be:
	    user friendly.
	    easy for staff and patrons to use.
	    equipped with useful prompts.
	    equipped with an introductory menu.
	    equipped with subsequent menus.
	    equipped with attractive and uncluttered screen
	        interfaces.		

G-28	support interlibrary loan for future transactions		
G-29	support an online union catalog of bibliographic records in brief and full U.S. MARC/MicroLIF Protocol format.		
G-30	be expandable.		
G-31	generate a variety of statistics and other reports and allow staff to customize reports. (Please supply samples of predefined reports.)		
G-32	be in full compliance with Z39.50 standard.		
G-33	permit downloading data from and onto floppy diskettes.		

Continued on next page

Figure 4.1 General essential specifications (continued).

Codes for Column 3:   A = Available   N = Not available   U = Under development
F = Future development

Scale for Column 4   1–5:   1 = Very poor   5 = Excellent

Note: The term *must* means essential.

Feature Number	The system must:	Code: A-N-U-F	Scale: 1–5
G-34	be augmented to support CD-ROM databases, access to the Internet, and other software and databases.		
G-35	provide ease of movement among the various modules with a function key/command in addition to menus.		
G-36	allow exit of modules with a single command/function key in addition to menus.		
G-37	have a fast response time, especially in a LAN environment. Please specify the response time for the following functions supported by a 586 micro-processor with a clock speed of 133 MHz: saving a cataloged record in a full U.S. MARC/MicroLIF Protocol. downloading 50 U.S. MARC/MicroLIF Protocol records from a floppy diskette. filing 50 newly cataloged or downloaded records. building keywords for 50 newly downloaded records. building 50 newly created cross references. searching by two keywords with the Boolean operator OR in OPAC. searching by two keywords with the Boolean operator AND in OPAC. searching by two keywords with the Boolean operator NOT in OPAC. searching with nested logic using more than three Boolean operators.		
G-38	include a screen saver, with time out adjustable by staff.		
G-39	allow patrons to access OPAC only, without a password.		
G-40	allow printing to a screen and a printer.		
G-41	provide full-screen editing for input data.		
G-42	interface with bibliographic utilities, such as the Georgia Online Database (GOLD) and OCLC.		
G-43	**The vendor must:** provide technical support through a toll-free telephone number between the hours of 7 a.m. and 6 p.m. Eastern Standard Time with response to calls within one hour.		

Continued on next page

Figure 4.1   **General essential specifications (continued).**

Feature Number	The system must:	Code: A-N-U-F	Scale: 1–5
G-44	be able to dial into the media center/library's file server via a modem to diagnose and troubleshoot problems.		
G-45	be able to communicate by e-mail and support a listserv on the Internet.		
G-46	provide frequent updates and enhancements of the software at no additional charge.		
G-47	provide on-site training in system use.		
G-48	supply a full set of documentation upon system installation.		
G-49	maintain clear, well-written, well-organized, and easy-to-use documentation. The documentation must have tabs with headings, explain the operation of the entire system, and provide instructions with examples and illustrations for each module. It must also be easy to update and include both a glossary and an alphabetical index.		
G-50	have qualified, well-trained, and friendly technical support and technical processing staff.		

This space is provided for vendor comments and explanation. Please use additional sheets if needed. **Refer to features by the feature number (column 1).**

Figure 4.2	**Essential specifications for utilities.**

Codes for Column 3:   A = Available   N = Not available   U = Under development
F = Future development

Scale for Column 4   1–5:   1 = Very poor   5 = Excellent

Note: The term *must* means essential.

Feature Number	The system must:	Code: A-N-U-F	Scale: 1–5
U-1	support full system backup.		
U-2	allow full system restoration from backup.		
U-3	permit setting backup date and time.		
U-4	support setting up multilevel passwords.		
U-5	enable setting up material and patron barcodes.		

U-6	allow:
	    addition and deletion of material and patron
	        barcodes.
	    editing of material and patron barcodes.		

U-7	support setting up the media center's or library's site information.		
	enable identification and set up of printers.		
	allow set up of modem type and baud rate.		

U-10	provide backup for:
	    acquisitions files.
	    cataloging files.
	    circulation files.
	    interlibrary loan files.
	    inventory data.
	    patron files.
	    serials files.		

U-11	restore backup files as needed.		
U-12	support setting keyword indexing based on MARC tags.		
U-13	allow activation/deactivation of specific keywords.		
U-14	support building/rebuilding keywords.		
U-15	allow update of keywords.		
U-16	allow global deletion of patron messages.		
U-17	support global deletion of material messages.		

U18	enable creation of user-defined indexes for:
	    materials (with author, title, call number, etc.).
	    patrons (with name, address, barcode, etc.).		

Continued on next page

| Figure 4.2 | **Essential specifications for utilities (continued).** |

Feature Number	The system must:	Code A-N-U-F	Scale 1–5

U-19	allow customization of:
	    screen colors.
	    help screens.
	    all types of reports.		

U-20	support setting up and editing of:
	    patron types.
	    material types.
	    locations for barcodes for media centers or libraries
	        in a union catalog.		

U-21	rebuild data files and indexes (e.g., author, titles, subject, etc.).		
U-22	print selected or all database files (e.g., circulation, cataloging, etc.).		
U-23	index/reindex the database.		
U-24	build/rebuild the database.		
U-25	build/rebuild authority records.		
U-26	build/rebuild keywords.		
U27	support saving all files, reports, and statistics.		
U-28	support setting up the inventory with a hand-held device.		

U-29	generate records processed for database files to include, but not limited to:
	    patron types.
	    fines.
	    statistics.
	    MARC records.
	    keywords built.
	    other (please specify).		

U-30	provide easy software installation.		
U-31	allow privacy option in OPAC to be turned on and off.		
U-32	support setting up and editing the calendar.		
U-33	diagnose installation problems and provide means for remediation.		

This space is provided for vendor comments and explanation. Please use additional sheets if needed. **Refer to features by the feature number (column 1).**

Figure 4.3   Essential specifications for cataloging.

Codes for Column 3:   A = Available   N = Not available   U = Under development
                      F = Future development

Scale for Column 4   1–5:   1 = Very poor   5 = Excellent

Note: The term *must* means essential.

Feature Number	The system must:	Code: A-N-U-F	Scale: 1–5
C-1	have a separate module for cataloging.		
C-2	function independently from other modules.		
C-3	function concurrently with other modules.		
C-4	support cataloging in real time (e.g., online).		
C-5	file newly cataloged or downloaded records in real time.		
C-6	construct indexes automatically and make them available for access immediately after filing.		
C-7	provide ease of movement among modules without re-login.		
C-8	support: AACR2R. all MARC designators (e.g., the Leader, the fixed field, variable data fields, and tags from 000 to 900). brief and full U.S. MARC and U.S. MARC/MicroLIF Protocol standards. ISBD.		
C-9	allow truncation and wild-character searching.		
C-10	maintain a single master bibliographic record with item records attached to it.		
C-11	provide error detection, especially before filing new records.		
C-12	allow members in an online union catalog to retain their own holdings and shelf location.		
C-13	permit global update, editing, and deletion of existing and imported records.		
C-14	support searching by: author. title. subject. keyword (from author, title, subject, series, and notes fields). Boolean operators (AND, OR, NOT). ISBN. ISSN. LCCN. type of material. other (please specify).		

Continued on next page

Figure 4.3	Essential specifications for cataloging (continued).

Feature Number	The system must:	Code: A-N-U-F	Scale 1–5
C-15	support magnetic tape or disk backup for all files in the database.		
C-16	create item records for circulation automatically, based on cataloged and downloaded records.		
C-17	allow addition of a copy of a record to support multiple copies and multivolume items.		
C-18	support addition of barcodes for multiple copies and multivolume items.		
C-19	provide online flexible editing capabilities that do not require going from a data entry mode to an editing mode. Editing must be supported for any data field without retyping the entire line or data field.		
C-20	transfer changes in the union catalog to local sites and vice versa.		
C-21	support merging records from commercial vendors with locally created records in order to provide full records for an online union catalog.		
C-22	disallow modification of files by unauthorized personnel.		
C-23	disallow saving a record without input in tag fields 100 to 500.		
C-24	support the display of a cataloged record on the screen before printing.		
C-25	provide an alert for record deletion if the circulation transaction is active on copies.		
C-26	customize and generate lists with fields and headings defined by staff to include, but not limited to: a printed catalog of books a separate printed catalog of audiovisual materials for each media center and for all media centers in a union catalog. new titles added, etc. for each media center and for all media centers in a Union Catalog. serials		
C-27	disallow deletion of records if any copies remain attached to a record.		
C-28	update all appropriate index entries automatically as changes are made in item and copy records, or as these records are deleted from the database.		

Continued on next page

Figure 4.3   **Essential specifications for cataloging (continued).**

Codes for Column 3:   A = Available   N = Not available   U = Under development
                      F = Future development

Scale for Column 4   1–5:   1 = Very poor   5 = Excellent

Note: The term *must* means essential.

Feature Number	The system must:	Code: A-N-U-F	Scale 1–5
C-29	support Dewey Decimal Classification call numbers.		
C-30	support *Sears List of Subject Headings*.		
C-31	allow manual keying of records and: addition of diacritical marks. addition and deletion of subfields. addition and deletion of tags.		
C-32	define each element in the Leader and fixed field of the MARC record in a pop-up window format or in a labeled format as the cursor is pointed at an element.		
C-33	provide an end-of-the line word wrapping feature to avoid sentence truncation.		
C-34	allow the title of a previously cataloged record to be copied for a new title edition, software version, etc.		
C-35	display records in a card catalog format in OPAC.		
C-36	support complete database maintenance and generate reports to include, but not limited to: new titles. titles with duplicate ISBN, ISSN, and/or LCCN. titles without ISBN, ISSN, and/or LCCN. updated titles.		
C-37	provide automatic daily back-up or alert operator to backup before exiting.		
C-38	support cataloging of a variety of types of materials in a U.S. MARC/MicroLIF Protocol format to include, but not limited to: books. CD-ROM. films, filmstrips, etc. videos. kits. laserdiscs. sound recordings (e.g., music CD, etc.). other media (please specify).		
C-39	support setting up the type of materials as default for original cataloging.		

Continued on next page

| Figure 4.3 | Essential specifications for cataloging (continued). | | |

Feature Number	The system must:	Code: A-N-U-F	Scale 1–5

C-40	generate, save, and print partial and full reports for the following fields:
	    author.
	    ISBN
	    shelflist.
	    subject.
	    title.		

C-41	allow printing proof sheets of a MARC record before saving.		
C-42	provide password protection.		

C-43	support complete database set up and customization to include, but not limited to:
	    apply and delete LC classification number.
	    apply and delete LC subject headings.
	    apply and delete local subject headings.
	    apply and delete *Sears* subject headings.
	    define field tags for brief MARC records.
	    delete LC classification number.
	    other (please describe).		

C-44	allow global addition of periods lacking at the end of authors' names and subject headings.		
C-45	allow batch downloading of MARC records from commercial sources and CD-ROM databases (e.g., Alliance Plus, Bibliofile, Precision One, etc.).		
C-46	zap imported records with existing records in the database to avoid duplication		
C-47	display duplicate records for review.		
C-48	transfer records from a U.S. MARC to a U.S. MARC/MicroLIF Protocol format.		

C-49	allow export of MARC records on floppy diskettes and magnetic tapes in both brief and full formats by a variety of methods to include:
	    author.
	    barcode.
	    combined features.
	    call number.
	    LCCN.
	    subject.
	    title.		

C-50	support large field sizes for data entry to avoid record truncation.		

Continued on next page

Figure 4.3   **Essential specifications for cataloging (continued).**

Codes for Column 3:   A = Available   N = Not available   U = Under development
                        F = Future development
Scale for Column 4   1–5:   1 = Very poor   5 = Excellent
Note: The term *must* means essential.

Feature Number	The system must:	Code: A-N-U-F	Scale 1–5
C-51	allow selection of MARC fields for keyword indexing.		
C-52	label each tag in a MARC record.		
C-53	display and print a blank MARC record.		
C-54	allow fields to be locally defined (e.g., 900 for local call number).		
C-55	allow addition of the following information to each MARC record: acquisition barcode copy and volume number fund price vendor name other information (please describe).		

This space is provided for vendor comments and explanation. Please use additional sheets if needed. **Refer to features by the feature number (column 1).**

Figure 4.4   Essential specifications for authority control.

Codes for Column 3:   A = Available   N = Not available   U = Under development
F = Future development

Scale for Column 4   1–5:   1 = Very poor   5 = Excellent

Note: The term *must* means essential.

Feature Number	The system must:	Code: A-N-U-F	Scale: 1–5
A-1	interface with cataloging and OPAC.		
A-2	function independently from other modules.		
A-3	provide a separate module for authority control that conforms to U.S. MARC format.		
A-4	support authority control for: author. series. subject. title.		
A-5	protect against the deletion of authorities that are still attached to bibliographic records.		
A-6	allow online maintenance of all fields in individual authority records.		
A-7	be compatible with the Library of Congress CD-ROM authority database (i.e., LC Names, LC Subjects, LC Titles) and accept authority records from external sources.		
A-8	allow creation of authority records online.		
A-9	allow editing of authority records online.		
A-10	allow deletion of authority records online.		
A-11	display problems with matches of headings against authority records when authorities are merged or changed.		
A-12	support *see* and *see also* references.		
A-13	flag or disallow blind references.		
A-14	relink modified authorities to their respective titles.		
A-15	allow searching of authority records by: author. series. subject. title.		
A-16	match each heading in the online catalog to authority records.		
A-17	set no limit on the number of authorities that can be linked to a bibliographic record.		
A-18	allow manual maintenance of all fields of authority records online.		

Continued on next page

Figure 4.4   Essential specifications for authority control (continued).

Feature Number	The system must:	Code: A-N-U-F	Scale: 1–5
A-19	provide an alert if a field that is about to be edited is an authority-controlled field.		
A-20	allow media centers/libraries in a union catalog to merge their authority records.		
A-21	allow global editing of authority records online.		
A-22	save authority records.		
A-23	print authority records alphabetically by: author. series. subject. title.		
A-24	print *see* and *see also* references.		
A-25	disallow saving and exiting authority records without information input in the following fields, as applicable: geographical subject headings (tag 151). fixed field (tag 008). Leader. main entry for corporate name (tag 110). main entry for personal name (tag 100). topical subject heading (tag 150). other headings (please describe).		
A-26	generate and print partial and full reports, in alphabetical order, for: name *see* headings. name *see also* headings. subject *see* headings. subject *see also* headings. series *see* headings. series *see also* headings.		
A-27	direct users from authorized headings to additional authorized headings for similar topics, and from unauthorized headings to authorized headings through cross-references.		
A-28	allow authorities for withdrawn items to be purged if no other items are attached to the authorities.		
A-29	display *see* and *see also* references in OPAC immediately after references are established.		
A-30	detect discrepancies between headings in bibliographic records and the headings in authority records.		
A-31	allow insertion of tags, subfields, and diacritical marks.		
A-32	provide password protection.		

This space is provided for vendor comments and explanation. Please use additional sheets if needed. **Refer to features by the feature number (column 1).**

Figure 4.5 **Essential specifications for OPAC.**

Codes for Column 3:   A = Available   N = Not available   U = Under development
F = Future development

Scale for Column 4   1–5:   1 = Very poor   5 = Excellent

Note: The term *must* means essential.

Feature Number	The system must:	Code: A-N-U-F	Scale: 1–5
O-1	function concurrently with other modules in the system.		
O-2	function independently from other modules.		
O-3	allow searching by: a combination of search indexes (e.g., author/title, author/subject, etc.). author. barcode number. Boolean operators (AND, OR, NOT). call number. ISBN. ISSN. key phrase. keyword in author, title, subject, content notes, and series. LCCN. subject. theme or material categories. title.		
O-4	support use of truncation and wild character in search statements to enhance information retrieval.		
O-5	permit users to limit searches by: publication date. type of materials. intellectual and grade level. other levels (please specify).		
O-6	maintain two modes of searching: one for novice, inexperienced users (menu-driven) and another for advanced, experienced users (command-driven). (Please provide examples of searches in both modes.)		
O-7	allow nesting or provide automatic, intelligent nesting of search statements. (Please provide examples of nesting.)		
O-8	alert users about searches requiring a long time to process and suggest alternative methods of search refinement.		
O-9	perform fast processing of searches with nesting, especially when more than three Boolean operators are used.		
O-10	provide an alphabetical list of keywords and allow browsing and selecting from the list.		

Continued on next page

Figure 4.5   Essential specifications for OPAC (continued).

Codes for Column 3:   A = Available   N = Not available   U = Under development
F = Future development

Scale for Column 4   1–5:   1 = Very poor   5 = Excellent

Note: The term *must* means essential.

Feature Number	The system must:	Code: A-N-U-F	Scale: 1–5
O-11	allow querying the system in both menu and command modes.		
O-12	support modification of search strategy.		
O-13	alert users about incorrect search parameters and provide means for remediation.		
O-14	ignore special diacritical marks and lower- and upper-case letters.		
O-15	forgive variations in punctuation and spacing.		
O-16	retrieve the "closest match" or provide a "sounds-like" feature in case of error in spelling or other type of error.		
O-17	disallow "no hits" and link a search statement to results in the union catalog in case of no hits in the local media center or library.		
O-18	retain users' search history on the screen.		
O-19	provide brief and full record display.		
O-20	allow users to terminate searches, especially long ones, easily and quickly.		
O-21	permit users to combine sets of search results.		
O-22	employ a list of stop words and allow users to display it any time during a search session.		
O-23	ignore stop words in search statements or alert users about removal of stop words from search statements.		
O-24	allow customization of screens (especially blocking certain features), displays, print functions, etc.		
O-25	provide different screen designs for keyword searching that support novice and experienced users, or allow the operator to customize them as necessary.		
O-26	support adjacent or proximity searching. (Please describe the proximity operators used.)		
O-27	provide an online tutorial with meaningful examples of various kinds of searching. Context-sensitive online assistance must be available within all searches.		
O-28	return to a summary screen when a search yields more than one hit.		
O-29	allow browsing by complete call number (or part of one) and display a list of entries in call number order.		

Continued on next page

Figure 4.5   **Essential specifications for OPAC (continued).**

Feature Number	The system must:	Code: A-N-U-F	Scale: 1–5
O-30	permit users to select an entry by highlighting it and pressing the Enter/Return key, or by pressing the number of the desired entry.		
O-31	support setting the default display of an entry in a traditional card catalog format, a labeled card catalog format, or other format.		
O-32	allow searching by: full author name in direct and indirect order. full subject in direct and indirect order. full title. partial author name in direct and indirect order. partial subject in direct and indirect order. words in title.		
O-33	match user search statements, in either direct or indirect format, with the standard correct format and retrieve information accordingly.		
O-34	sort search results in a variety of methods (e.g., alphabetically by author, title, subject, etc.).		
O-35	print search results on the screen and save them on floppy diskettes, as needed.		
O-36	allow cancellation of saved searches.		
O-37	provide automatic flip or display of *see* and *see also* references on the screen based on authority records.		
O-38	display search results in a MARC format at the option of the user.		
O-39	permit paging and scrolling backward and forward easily within all searches.		
O-40	display the local titles, holdings, and locations from the media center or library where a search is conducted.		
O-41	display the titles, holdings, and locations of media centers or libraries in a union catalog at the option of the user. A command or a function key for union catalog access must be present when results are displayed.		
O-42	display the status of an item retrieved, such as: at the bindery. available. in circulation (with due date). in-processing. missing, lost, etc. on-order. on reserve. received. other (please specify).		

Continued on next page

Figure 4.5   Essential specifications for OPAC (continued).

Codes for Column 3:   A = Available   N = Not available   U = Under development
                      F = Future development

Scale for Column 4   1–5:   1 = Very poor   5 = Excellent

Note: The term *must* means essential.

Feature Number	The system must:	Code: A-N-U-F	Scale: 1–5
O-43	support limiting the number of citations to be printed.		
O-44	display search results in alphabetical order.		
O-45	display the number of postings for each search statement on the screen.		
O-46	provide remote access to OPAC.		
O-47	support backup of the OPAC database as needed.		
O-48	support restoration of the OPAC database as needed.		
O-49	allow specification of the fields to be keyword indexed.		
O-50	support the compilation and customization of bibliographies. Allow bibliography listings to be displayed on the screen for review before printing.		
O-51	provide search use statistics for: annual transactions for types of searches. (Please provide samples of search use statistics.) monthly transactions for types of searches. types of searches (e.g., author, title, subject, etc.) in novice and advanced search modes.		
O-52	allow turning search limiters on and off.		
O-53	disregard initial articles in the beginning of a search statement.		
O-54	return to the beginning of the search process when requested or after a reasonable timeout. (Please specify the timeout feature.)		
O-55	provide meaningful and easy-to-follow prompts throughout the search process.		
O-56	disallow users from accessing other modules in the system.		
O-57	be user-friendly and easy to use.		

This space is provided for vendor comments and explanation. Please use additional sheets if needed. **Refer to features by the feature number (column 1).**

Figure 4.6   **Essential specifications for circulation.**

Codes for Column 3:   A = Available   N = Not available   U = Under development
F = Future development

Scale for Column 4   1–5:   1 = Very poor   5 = Excellent

Note: The term *must* means essential.

Feature Number	The system must:	Code: A-N-U-F	Scale: 1–5
CR-1	support brief and full U.S. MARC and U.S. MARC/MicroLIF Protocol standards.		
CR-2	support all circulation functions, including: check-in. check-out. fines. inventory. overdues. renewal. reports. reserve/hold. statistics.		
CR-3	function with other modules in the system.		
CR-4	function independently from other modules in the system.		
CR-5	display item status in OPAC.		
CR-6	provide security through multiple password protection.		
CR-7	provide an alert about records that are about to be deleted.		
CR-8	confirm deletion of records.		
CR-9	support partial and full inventory via a hand-held device.		
CR-10	accept manual keying and optical scanning of barcodes.		
CR-11	maintain a calendar and provide control for holidays and closing days.		
CR-12	support a minimum of 40 patron categories and 99 material types.		
CR-13	allow fines and due dates to vary with material codes and borrower types.		
CR-14	support renewal in a separate function.		
CR-15	allow customization of reports.		
CR-16	keep statistics for a minimum of two years.		
CR-17	support creation of borrower and item records on the fly.		
CR-18	support reserve/hold in a separate function.		

Continued on next page

Figure 4.6   **Essential specifications for circulation (continued).**

Codes for Column 3:   A = Available   N = Not available   U = Under development
F = Future development

Scale for Column 4   1–5:   1 = Very poor   5 = Excellent

Note: The term *must* means essential.

Feature Number	The system must:	Code: A-N-U-F	Scale: 1–5
CR-19	allow patron records to be downloaded from another source (e.g., a student management database, especially OSIRIS).		
CR-20	support updating the database online.		
CR-21	allow customization of the database.		
CR-22	allow staff to define and override loan periods.		
CR-23	support global editing of records.		
CR-24	support global deletion of records.		
CR-25	provide a circulation log for various types of materials.		
CR-26	provide an audible or visual signal when a transaction is completed.		
CR-27	provide a good menu- or command-driven user interface with uncluttered screen design.		
CR-28	support context-sensitive help or a help index that is always present on all screens.		
CR-29	allow searching of patron records by: barcode number. patron ID number. patron name (first or last). other (please specify).		
CR-30	support initiation of a global due date in the entire database.		
CR-31	have a fast response time for all transactions. Please specify the response time for the following functions supported by a 586 microprocessor with a clock speed of 133 MHz: composing overdues and fines for 50 items. generating a report of overdues and fines for 50 items. generating an inventory report for 50 scanned items. generating a payment receipt. scanning 50 barcode numbers at check-out and check-in. scanning 50 barcode numbers using an inventory scanner.		
CR-32	support customization of a patron database by renaming the various fields.		

Continued on next page

Figure 4.6 **Essential specifications for circulation (continued).**

Feature Number	The system must:	Code: A-N-U-F	Scale: 1–5
CR-33	accommodate a database of a minimum of 50,000 patron records and support its future growth to a minimum of 100,000.		
CR-34	support limiting the number of items circulated based on item category and patron type.		
CR-35	allow addition of fees to a patron record for damaged items, lost copies, etc.		
CR-36	calculate loan periods and due dates automatically according to: closing days. material type. patron status or category. other (please specify).		
CR-37	support variation in loan periods and due dates.		
CR-38	verify patron eligibility for item check-out.		
CR-39	maintain blocking features or traps.		
CR-40	alert staff about blocking features or traps at check-out.		
CR-41	accept and forgive partial and full fines.		
CR-42	allow due dates to be changed online.		
CR-43	display a patron history for items checked out online, along with the titles checked out, overdues, etc.		
CR-44	support a brief entry of a patron name, and provide a browsing list of names in alphabetical order.		
CR-45	provide an alert when a barcode is invalid, scanned, or keyed in incorrectly.		
CR-46	display the due dates and titles of items on the terminal screen at the time of check-out.		
CR-47	maintain confidentiality of patron records, especially when item availability is displayed in OPAC.		
CR-48	support material check-out from any terminal.		
CR-49	allow multiple item check-out on a single ID.		
CR-50	place items back in circulation immediately after check-in.		
CR-51	provide an alert when a returned item does not belong to the local media center or library.		
CR-52	support item check-in or check-out using a barcode scanner.		
CR-53	support item check-in or check-out by keying in the barcode.		

Continued on next page

Figure 4.6 Essential specifications for circulation (continued).

Codes for Column 3:   A = Available   N = Not available   U = Under development
F = Future development

Scale for Column 4   1–5:   1 = Very poor   5 = Excellent

Note: The term *must* means essential.

Feature Number	The system must:	Code: A-N-U-F	Scale: 1–5
CR-54	signal hold/reserve or other conditions at the time of check-in.		
CR-55	calculate overdues at the time of check-in and attach a fine to a patron record automatically.		
CR-56	support material check-in from any terminal.		
CR-57	give an audible or visual signal when a transaction is completed.		
CR-58	disengage an item from a patron record at check-in unless a fine is attached.		
CR-59	support fine control and print overdue notices in a variety of sequences.		
CR-60	provide a separate renewal function.		
CR-61	block renewal if an item is on hold.		
CR-62	block renewal if an item is overdue.		
CR-63	calculate and display new dates for renewals.		
CR-64	allow item renewal without scanning the item barcode (e.g., by phone).		
CR-65	produce a chronological queue for items on hold/reserve.		
CR-66	allow overriding a chronological queue for items on hold/reserve.		
CR-67	cancel a hold on an item automatically when the item is checked out, unless the item is on hold for other patrons in the queue. In the latter case, it must readjust the hold queue.		
CR-68	cancel a hold on an item when the item is not claimed within a designated period of time.		
CR-69	cancel a hold on an item when an item is indicated lost or missing.		
CR-70	compose and print the following notices: hold. overdue. recall. renewal. other (please specify).		

Continued on next page

Figure 4.6   **Essential specifications for circulation (continued).**

Feature Number	The system must:	Code: A-N-U-F	Scale: 1–5

CR-71	create a patron record with the following information:
	    barcode number.
	    classification code.
	    full address.
	    full name.
	    ID expiration date.
	    ID or Social Security number.
	    location or homeroom number.
	    status or classification.
	    telephone number.
	    other (please specify).		

CR-72	support online editing or revision of information in a patron record.		
CR-73	print overdue reports for fines that are forgiven, partially paid, or paid in full.		

CR-74	sort overdue reports by:
	    call number of item.
	    patron address.
	    patron ID number.
	    patron location or homeroom number.
	    patron name.
	    title of item.		

CR-75	calculate fines for damaged or lost items.		
CR-76	support waiving fines.		
CR-77	with one keystroke print receipts for fines and fees paid.		

CR-78	include the following information for overdue notices:
	    author(s) of item(s).
	    call number of item(s).
	    date notice was prepared.
	    due date(s) of items.
	    patron address or homeroom number.
	    patron grade level.
	    patron ID number.
	    patron name.
	    title of item(s).
	    other (please specify).		

CR-79	allow customization of the format and content of overdue lists or reports.		
CR-80	generate a list of lost or damaged items.		

CR-81	provide circulation statistics for a variety of circulation activities:
	    biweekly.
	    daily.
	    monthly.
	    weekly.
	    other frequency (please specify).		

Continued on next page

Figure 4.6   Essential specifications for circulation (continued).

Codes for Column 3:   A = Available   N = Not available   U = Under development
F = Future development

Scale for Column 4   1–5:   1 = Very poor   5 = Excellent

Note: The term *must* means essential.

Feature Number	The system must:	Code: A-N-U-F	Scale: 1–5
CR-82	purge cleared transactions regularly, but retain the statistical data for management purposes.		
CR-83	save statistical reports.		
CR-84	provide circulation statistics and statistical reports for: blocked patrons. items lost and paid for. items never circulated. items on hold. list of deleted barcode numbers. list of patrons with expired cards. lost items. total fines paid to date. total number of items checked out to date.		
CR-85	provide circulation statistics and statistical reports for a variety of circulation activities by: a combination of all or some of the above. call number. grade level. homeroom number or other location. locally defined codes or categories. patron status or category. type of material.		
CR-86	list items previously reported lost but currently are on the shelves or in the circulation file.		
CR-87	print inventory reports for missing items, misshelved items, etc., in order by call number.		
CR-88	support partial and full inventory of materials.		
CR-89	print statistical reports based on locally defined formats.		
CR-90	provide detailed statistical reports for all circulation activities on a: annual basis. daily basis. monthly basis.		
CR-91	display statistical reports online before printing.		
CR-92	determine material use by: Dewey classification numbers. patron status or category. type of material. other (please describe).		

This space is provided for vendor comments and explanation. Please use additional sheets if needed. **Refer to features by the feature number (column 1).**

Figure 4.7 **Essential specifications for acquisitions.**

Codes for Column 3: A = Available N = Not available U = Under development
F = Future development

Scale for Column 4 1–5: 1 = Very poor 5 = Excellent

Note: The term *must* means essential.

Feature Number	The system must:	Code: A-N-U-F	Scale: 1–5
AC-1	function concurrently with other modules in the system.		
AC-2	function independently of other modules in the system.		
AC-3	support various acquisitions functions, including: material requests. purchase orders. receiving. claiming. cancellation. verification of items against outstanding orders. verification of items against existing materials in OPAC. budget and fund accounting.		
AC-4	interface online with material suppliers to support ordering, inquiries, claiming, and other related tasks.		
AC-5	allow searching of records by: author. title. publication date. ISBN. LCCN. publisher name. purchase order number. order date. requester's name. vendor's or supplier's name. fund code.		
AC-6	prepare and print: purchase orders. invoices. payment vouchers.		
AC-7	allow : customization of purchase orders. encumbrance of funds. adjustment of funds as material receipt is input. creation of new accounts.		
AC-8	provide an alert about insufficient funds for ordering.		

Continued on next page

| Figure 4.7 | Essential specifications for acquisitions (continued). |

Codes for Column 3: A = Available N = Not available U = Under development
                     F = Future development

Scale for Column 4   1–5: 1 = Very poor   5 = Excellent

Note: The term *must* means essential.

Feature Number	The system must:	Code: A-N-U-F	Scale: 1–5
AC-9	support overcommitments of funds.		
AC-10	support multiple fund codes for media centers or libraries in a union catalog.		
AC-11	allow multiple copies to be ordered for multiple media centers or libraries in the union catalog.		
AC-12	allow deletion of vendor records online.		
AC-13	support one order for multiple copies.		
AC-14	automatically display acquisitions status in OPAC as item status is modified.		
AC-15	support reviewing all orders online before printing or sending them electronically.		
AC-16	generate a list of materials not received within a set time period.		
AC-17	track materials not received within a set time period.		

AC-18	maintain a file to include information about each vendor and facilitate material acquisition. Vendor file must include:
	    account number.
	    address.
	    name.
	    fax number.
	    telephone number.		

AC-19	store full and partial acquisitions records with the following information:
	    author.
	    cost.
	    fund code.
	    ISBN.
	    number of copies requested.
	    publication date.
	    title.
	    type of binding.
	    vendor name.
	    other (please specify).		

AC-20	permit setting and changing the timing for cancellation.		

Continued on next page

Figure 4.7	**Essential specifications for acquisitions (continued).**

Feature Number	The system must:	Code: A-N-U-F	Scale: 1–5
AC-21	issue claims for materials not received within a set time period, change the status from "on order" to "claimed," and provide the date of the claim.		
AC-22	support cancellation of orders and allow transfer of canceled orders to another vendor file to issue new orders.		
AC-23	print cancellation notices, lists, or letters to both vendors and requesters.		
AC-24	change item status from "on order" to "canceled" and provide the date of cancellation.		
AC-25	change item status from "on order" to "received" and provide the date of receipt.		
AC-26	track vendor performance and provide performance statistics.		
AC-27	prepare budget reports with funds encumbered, spent, and available.		
AC-28	set back funds to zero at the end of the fiscal year.		
AC-29	keep statistics for a minimum of two years.		
AC-30	provide password protection.		
AC-31	support database backup and restoration.		
AC-32	prepare and generate statistical reports for the following: canceled items. claimed items. items not yet received. items on order. received items. returned items. unavailable items (e.g., out-of-print, etc.). other. (Please describe and provide samples of reports.)		

This space is provided for vendor comments and explanation. Please use additional sheets if needed. **Refer to features by the feature number (column 1).**

Figure 4.8   **Essential specifications for serials.**

Codes for Column 3:   A = Available   N = Not available   U = Under development
                      F = Future development

Scale for Column 4   1–5:   1 = Very poor   5 = Excellent

Note: The term *must* means essential.

Feature Number	The system must:	Code: A-N-U-F	Scale: 1–5
S-1	function concurrently with other modules in the system.		
S-2	function independently of other modules in the system.		
S-3	support various serials functions, including: bindery management. budget and fund accounting. cancellation. check-in. claiming. ordering. renewal. routing.		
S-4	manage and maintain serials holdings.		
S-5	accommodate all types of serials, including but not limited to: annuals or yearbooks. journals and magazines. newspapers. periodical indexes.		
S-6	accommodate various frequencies as well as special and irregular issues.		
S-7	adjust changes in frequencies, titles, publishers, etc.		
S-8	produce routing slips.		
S-9	interface online with serials vendors to support electronic ordering, inquiries, claiming, and other related tasks.		
S-10	support reviewing all orders online before printing or sending them electronically.		
S-11	allow searching by: Boolean operators. CODEN. date of first issue. ISSN. keyword. other dates. publisher. title. vendor. other (please specify).		

Continued on next page

Figure 4.8 **Essential specifications for serials (continued).**

Feature Number	The system must:	Code: A-N-U-F	Scale: 1–5
S-12	store full and partial serials records with the following information: fund code. ISSN. subscription cost. title. vendor name. volume, issue, and date. other (please specify).		
S-13	support one order for multiple copies.		
S-14	support multiple fund codes for media centers or libraries in a union catalog.		
S-15	maintain a vendor file to include, but not limited to: account number. address. fax number. name. telephone number.		
S-16	support: encumbrance of funds. adjustment of funds as serials are received. creation of new accounts.		
S-17	allow multiple copies to be ordered for multiple members in the union catalog.		
S-18	provide an alert about insufficient funds for ordering.		
S-19	track volumes or issues not received within a set time period and generate claims automatically.		
S-20	prepare budget reports with funds encumbered, spent, and available.		
S-21	set back funds to zero at the end of the fiscal year.		
S-22	change the status of claimed serials from "on order" to "claimed," and provide the date of the claim.		
S-23	automatically display item status in OPAC as status is modified.		
S-24	support setting and changing the timing for cancellation.		
S-25	change item status from "on order" to "canceled," and provide the date of cancellation.		

Continued on next page

Figure 4.8   Essential specifications for serials (continued).

Codes for Column 3:   A = Available   N = Not available   U = Under development
F = Future development

Scale for Column 4   1–5:   1 = Very poor   5 = Excellent

Note: The term *must* means essential.

Feature Number	The system must:	Code: A-N-U-F	Scale: 1–5
S-26	allow input of messages about changes in serials titles, publishers, etc.		
S-27	prepare and generate statistical reports for the following: 　　received items. 　　canceled items. 　　renewed items 　　claimed items. 　　routed items. 　　items not yet received. 　　items on order. 　　other. (Please describe and provide samples of reports.)		
S-28	keep statistics for a minimum of two years.		
S-29	track vendor performance and provide performance statistics.		
S-30	allow deletion of vendor records online.		

This space is provided for vendor comments and explanation. Please use additional sheets if needed. **Refer to features by the feature number (column 1).**

Figure 4.9 Essential specifications for hardware: file server.

Codes for Column 3:   A = Available   N = Not available   U = Under development
F = Future development

Scale for Column 4   1–5:   1 = Very poor   5 = Excellent

Note: The term *must* means essential.

Feature Number	The system must:	Code: A-N-U-F	Scale: 1–5
H-1	operate on MS-DOS version 6.5 or higher and be compatible with MS Windows version 3.1 or higher.		
H-2	be compatible with the automation software used and accommodate its workloads. (The media specialist or information professional should provide the name of the system and its workloads in this column.)		
H-3	have a 586 microprocessor with a minimum of 133 MHz clock speed or higher.		
H-4	have two small computer system Interface (SCSI) hot-swappable hard drives to protect against server crashes.		
H-5	have 4 GB of hard disk storage.		
H-6	have a minimum of 4,500 round per minute (rpm) hard disk.		
H-7	have 64 MB of RAM or higher.		
H-8	have 32 MB of network cache.		
H-9	have one high-density 3.5-inch disk drive.		
H-10	accommodate a tape backup with a high storage capacity. (Please specify the capacity.)		
H-11	have a 17-inch color monitor.		
H-12	accommodate an internal modem with 28,800 Kbps or higher.		
H-13	accommodate an uninterrupted power supply unit (UPS).		
H-14	have at least a 300-watt power supply to avoid overheating.		

H-15	have expansion capability for a minimum of:
	    four Extended Industry Standard Architecture
	        (EISA) open slots.
	    two Peripheral Control Interface (PCI) slots.
	    other slots (please describe).		

H-16	coexist with CD-towers in a LAN environment.		

Continued on next page

Figure 4.9 Essential specifications for hardware: file server (continued).

Codes for Column 3:   A = Available   N = Not available   U = Under development
                      F = Future development

Scale for Column 4   1–5:   1 = Very poor   5 = Excellent

Note: The term *must* means essential.

Feature Number	The system must:	Code: A-N-U-F	Scale: 1–5
H-17	be compatible with Novell Netware version 4.1 or higher.		
H-18	have a minimum 64-bit bus.		
H-19	support data stripping.		
H-20	accommodate a second central processing unit (CPU).		
H-21	be able to connect to the Internet and World Wide Web.		
H-22	support: monitoring or diagnosing the operations from a remote location. paging a network administrator as needed. rebooting or fixing problems from a remote location.		
H-23	be compatible with Windows NT in a networking environment, most likely Ethernet.		
H-24	accommodate a minimum of 50 client stations simultaneously.		
H-25	have software that supports: customized installation. diagnostics. EISA configuration. utilities (please specify).		
H-26	maintain hardware documentation both online and in printed format.		
H-27	be quiet and well cooled.		
H-28	provide tools for detecting and alerting about problems.		
H-29	have a dual power supply.		
H-30	support a network router.		
H-31	support a built-in, high-performance network adapter with high-speed access to the CPU and memory. (Please specify the kind of adapter(s) supported.)		
H-32	have a CD-ROM drive.		
H-33	have built-in security features (please describe).		

Continued on next page

Figure 4.9 **Essential specifications for hardware: file server (continued).**

Feature Number	The system must:	Code: A-N-U-F	Scale: 1–5
H-34	automatically reboot after a software crash or power failure.		
H-35	support mirroring of disk drives to avoid interruption of operations.		
H-36	**The vendor must provide:** access to own home page on the World Wide Web. a minimum of three-year on-site service warranty. documentation in printed format upon purchase. responses to problems within two hours from the initial call. support via e-mail. training as needed. troubleshooting and diagnosis via modem. 24-hour, toll-free technical support.		

This space is provided for vendor comments and explanation. Please use additional sheets if needed. **Refer to features by the feature number (column 1).**

5 Preparing the Collection for the Automated System

■ Implementation is the most time-consuming activity in any automation project. It entails a wide range of activities, including collection preparation, database creation through retrospective conversion (Recon), barcoding, site preparation, software installation, user training, and database management. Because it is such a big topic, it has been divided into two chapters for purposes of this discussion. This chapter describes the various stages and activities related to the collection itself. Chapter 6 deals with issues related to facilities, installation, and ongoing use and management. Although the discussion of these topics has been divided for purposes of this book, it is important to remember that an integrated automation system requires integrated implementation; the steps taken in preparing the collection will affect later stages of implementation, and how the system will be used and managed must be taken into account during collection preparation.

Implementation activities related to the collection itself are collection preparation, retrospective conversion, complying with bibliographic standards, and barcoding. Retrospective conversion is a key step in implementing an automated system. Simply put, Recon means converting the card catalog (or shelflist) into a database. (The shelflist is the part of the card catalog that contains one card for each item owned by the library; cards are arranged by a classification number, such as Dewey number.) This database supports the automated system (e.g., it is the basis of OPAC).

■ Collection Preparation

Collection preparation is an essential prerequisite for Recon. Adequate collection preparation—weeding, inventorying the collection, and analyzing the shelflist—saves both time and money in Recon.

☐ Weeding

Every media center or library should have a weeding policy or criteria to use in judging which materials are to be withdrawn, replaced, or repaired, as well as what to do with materials that are withdrawn from the collection. The policy or criteria should guide the staff in weeding the entire collection as a first step in preparing the collection for Recon.

After weeding is completed, shelflist cards for withdrawn items must be removed. Withdrawn materials may be discarded, exchanged with other media centers or libraries, or otherwise disposed of based on material disposition guidelines or policy.

In Recon, the vendor reviews the shelflist, matching each item in the shelflist against the MARC database. Usually, vendors charge for each item matched against the shelflist. By weeding, one reduces the number of items to be converted to machine-readable format and therefore reduces the cost of Recon. Weeding produces savings in time and money, even when Recon is performed in-house; weeding the collection before beginning Recon prevents staff from converting items that are not needed in the collection.

☐ Inventory

A thorough inventory is essential to identify items for which no shelflist cards exist and to identify shelflist cards for which materials are missing or lost. A decision should be made with regard to the kinds of materials to be converted (e.g., videos, kits, laserdiscs, magazines, serials). The inventory should then be performed on all materials to be converted. All materials that are destined for conversion must have shelflist cards.

☐ Shelflist Analysis

Shelflist analysis is performed to examine the completeness and accuracy of the shelflist, including variations in and consistency of items' call numbers, locations, and prefixes. All materials to be converted should have cards, and those cards should be as complete and accurate as possible. The more complete and accurate the cards are, the higher the probability is for finding matches. (As explained in more detail later, Recon is performed by matching shelflist cards against U.S. MARC databases, then copying the appropriate MARC records onto a disk. These records, put together, form the database on which the automated system is based.) The quality of Recon, whether in-house or off-site, begins with the accuracy and completeness of the shelflist. Therefore, adequate time should be devoted to cleaning up and standardizing the shelflist.

The benefits of a standardized shelflist go beyond Recon. Uniformity and consistency will serve patrons better by making information retrieval more effective, especially in a union catalog environment.

In analyzing the shelflist, make sure that each card contains the following information:

> accurate bibliographic information (e.g., author, title, publication information, etc.);
>
> a call number and a standard prefix (e.g., B 921 for individual biographies, R or REF for reference);
>
> number of copies, so that a barcode can be generated for each copy;
>
> number of volumes (for multivolume items), so that a barcode can be generated for each volume;
>
> complete bibliographic information, including notes, grade level, and subject headings;
>
> LCCN, ISBN, ISSN for each item, as applicable, including multivolume works and multiple copies;
>
> a circulation category; and
>
> a standardized location code.

■ Retrospective Conversion

Retrospective conversion involves converting a shelflist into a machine-readable format based on recognized bibliographic standards (i.e., U.S. MARC or U.S. MARC/MicroLIF Protocol) for the purpose of creating a database that supports the operation of an automated system. This is generally done by searching for each and every item in the shelflist in one or more standard bibliographic databases. Whenever a match is found—that is, whenever a record in the bibliographic database exactly matches the item in the shelflist—the record from the database is downloaded. These downloaded records form the database that supports the automated system.

☐ Specifications for Recon

Developing specifications for Recon allows one to customize the content of the automated system's MARC database and thus maintain consistency in its format. Specifications stipulate what to include and exclude from each MARC record and also identify which fields require editing, enhancement, or special attention. Regardless of the method of conversion used (vendor, in-house, or combination), specifications for Recon should be established. This will clarify for the vendor or in-house staff what is expected of them and will ensure that the finished product meets the needs and requirements of the media center or library. It also gives the vendor a profile of the institution's MARC records to use not only in performing Recon but also in filling future orders for MARC records (e.g., a media center might periodically order MARC records for newly purchased materials). Specifications may stipulate the following:

- Classification numbers: The number to include, exclude, verify, or edit (e.g., Dewey, Library of Congress, or both). A specification in this area may include, for example, that "Dewey numbers should be verified for their length and that long numbers should be simplified at the first prime mark."

- Subject headings: The headings to include, exclude, verify, or edit (e.g., *Sears,* Library of Congress, Library of Congress Children's List). A specification in this area may indicate, for example, "All subject headings must end with a period."

- Enhancements: The kinds of enhancements that need to be added to each record (e.g., detailed notes in MARC tag 521, grade level.) A specification in this area may state, "All MARC records must have the audience grade level in tag 521."

- Record format: The provision of full U.S. MARC or U.S. MARC/MicroLIF Protocol records based on *AACR2R* and ISBD standards. A specification in this area may state, "All records must comply with U.S. MARC/MicroLIF Protocol."

- Record content: The inclusion of the Leader and fixed field in each MARC record. Specifications in this area may also require provision of General Material Description (GMD) for all nonprint materials, the standard use of prefixes established for shelflist analysis (e.g., R for reference, B for biographies, Video for videotapes), and call numbers, among other things. A specification in this area may state, "GMD must be included for all nonprint materials."

- Recon databases: The extraction of MARC records from the Library of Congress (LC) database, contributors' databases, the Library of Canada database, and other databases. A specification in this area may state, "Only LC records are accepted" and "Nonmatched items should be keyed in manually."

- Accuracy rate: The matched records should be as accurate as possible. A specification in this case might state, "The accuracy rate of matched records must not fall below 90 percent."

Developing specifications for Recon requires adequate knowledge of the various components of a MARC record format. Knowledge of *AACR2R* is a prerequisite for understanding the MARC record and for maintaining consistency in the content of the MARC database.

☐ Retrospective Conversion: Who Does It?

A database can be created off-site by an automation vendor, in-house by a media specialist or information professional or trained staff, or by a combination of staff. Each option has advantages and disadvantages. Selecting an option depends on the cost, the knowledge and skill of the staff who will carry out the conversion in-house, staffing levels, and the amount of time allocated for implementing the automation project.

Vendor Conversion Process

This process requires that a shelflist be prepared, packed, and shipped based on the guidelines provided by the Recon vendor. (It is highly recommended that the shelflist be insured so that it can be tracked in case it is lost in shipping. If you send it "return receipt requested," you will know when it arrived at the vendor.) After receiving the shelflist, the vendor assigns one or more operators to perform the conversion.

The procedure for converting the shelflist is fairly straightforward. An operator searches one or more master U.S. MARC databases to find a match for each shelflist card. Searches are done by LCCN, ISBN, or other standard parameter. Matched MARC records are saved on diskettes (to be sent to the media center or library). Some vendors edit and enhance the records. The vendor then links a barcode to each record; because this barcode identifies the linked record, it is called a smart barcode. Upon completion of Recon, the vendor returns the shelflist to the media center or library, along with the diskettes containing the MARC records and smart barcode labels.

Inevitably, some shelflist cards will not be matched in the U.S. MARC database; these records are either created manually by the vendor (operator) or the shelflist card is returned to the media center or library. Records for the returned cards can be created in-house after the cataloging database has been implemented, or they can be matched against a database of MARC records (possibly on CD-ROM) at a neighboring library or at the district library.

Advantages of Vendor Conversion

The vendor conversion process has the following advantages:

- It allows the media specialist or information professional to engage in other activities on site.

- It provides faster completion of database creation, first, because the operators are well versed in the procedure, and second, because the vendor may assign several full-time operators to work on the project. This is not likely to happen if Recon is done in-house.

- The turnaround time for completion of Recon can be predicted. This helps planners and managers establish a schedule for implementing the automated system.

- It may generate a high match rate, especially when more than one database is used.

- Records for unmatched items may be created by the operator, thus saving library staff time.

- Smart barcodes (i.e., barcodes containing the name of the media center or library, title of the item, call number, and other information, as specified) are supplied with converted items.

- Authority records may be linked to converted items.

Disadvantages of Vendor Conversion

The vendor conversion process has the following disadvantages:

- The conversion may not be completed on time as scheduled.

- The shelflist may be lost in transit.

- There is always a possibility of mismatches and errors. Database cleanup is highly recommended. This is performed after the MARC records (supplied by the vendor on diskettes) are downloaded into the cataloging database.

- The absence of the shelflist from the media center or library may make it difficult to answer some users' questions. For example, if a user needs information about an item, and that information is not provided on the item's catalog card—but it is provided on the shelflist card—then, in the absence of the shelflist, that user's question cannot be answered. A user may wish to know, for example, how many volumes of a particular work the library owns; this information may appear on the shelflist, but not on the catalog card.

Choosing a Vendor for Recon

Many companies offer Recon service. Follett Software Company, Winnebago Library Software Company, Brodart Automation, and Nichols Advanced Technologies, Inc., are just a few. Table 5.1 lists some important characteristics of various vendor conversion services. Table 5.2 lists some Recon and automation software vendors. In selecting a specific vendor, consider

- The MARC database used to extract the records. The Library of Congress database is preferred because of its authoritativeness.

- The size of the MARC databases consulted and the type of records included (e.g., print, nonprint). A vendor's database of LC MARC should contain more than 2 million records. (You may wish to include this as a criteria in selecting a Recon vendor.)

Table 5.1 **Characteristics of Recon Service Provided by Selected Vendors**

Vendor	Database	Charges*
Brodart Automation 500 Arch St. Williamsport, PA 17705 (800) 233-8467	Off-site:† Library of Congress (LC), Precision One, and other databases.	Based on shelflist samples.
	In-house: Precision One Cataloging.	$500 quarterly; $750 monthly.
COMPanion Corp. 1831 Fort Union Blvd. Salt Lake City, UT 84121 (800) 347-6439 (801) 943-7277	Off-site: Library of Congress (LC). Size: over 3 million.	$0.49 per each match and key-in. No enhancements.
	In-house: Smart MARC software and Precision One (CD-ROM).	$695.
Follett Software Company 1391 Corporate Dr. McHenry, IL 60050 (800) 323-3397 (815) 344-8700	Off-site: Library of Congress.	$0.58 per each match and key-in. Enhancements included.

Continued on next page

Table 5.1 **Characteristics of Recon Service Provided by Selected Vendors (continued).**

Vendor	Database	Charges*
Follett Software Company 1391 Corporate Dr. McHenry, IL 60050 (800) 323-3397 (815) 344-8700	In-house: Alliance Plus (CD-ROM). Alliance AV/Access (CD-ROM). Plus and Access combined.	$295. $595 per year. $1,040 per year.
The Library Corporation Research Park Inwood, WV 25428 (800) 325-7759	In-house: Bibliofile (Total of 13 databases). Size: 11 million records. LC MARC English. AV Access.	$22,000. $1,845 a year. $995 a year.
Library of Congress Cataloging Distribution Service Washington, DC 20542 (202) 707-6100	In-house: CD-MARC Bibliographic (4 million records). CD-MARC Names (2.4 million name authorities). CD-MARC Subjects (180,000 subject authorities).	$4,00 per year. $300 per year. $400 per year.
Nichols Advanced Technologies, Inc. 3452 Losey Blvd. South LaCrosse, WI 54601 (800) 658-9453 (608) 787-8333	Off-site: Library of Congress and contributors' databases.	$0.46 per each match or key-in. Extra for enhancement.
	In-house: Athena/CD Cataloger. MITINET/MARC.	$995 first year; $595 annual update. $399
SIRS Mandarin P.O. Box 2348 Boca Raton, FL 33427 (800) 232-SIRS (518) 298-2970	Off-site: Precision One.	$0.50 per each match. $0.60 per key-in. Extra for enhancement.
	In-house: MITINET/MARC	Free with software purchase.
Winnebago Library Software Company 457 E. South St. Caledonia, MN 55921 (800) 533-5430	Off-site: Library of Congress.	$0.39 per each match. $0.59 per key-in (full MARC). Extra for enhancement.
	In-house: Not applicable.	Not applicable.

*An initial set up fee may apply
†Performed by vendor.

Table 5.2 Selected Software Vendors

System	Vendor	Platform/Other
Bibliofile	The Library Corporation Research Park Inwood, WV 25428 (800) 325-7759 (304) 229-0100	DOS, Windows, NT, (CD-ROM-based) http://www.bibfile.com Z39.50 via Internet
CASPR	Caspr, Inc. 635 Vaqueros Ave. Sunnyvale, CA 94086 (800) 852-2777 (408) 522-9800	Mac, Windows, NT, DOS http://www.caspr.com
COMPanion Alexandria	COMPanion Corp. 1831 Fort Union Blvd. Salt Lake City, UT 84121 (800) 347-6439 (801) 943-7277	Mac, DOS (patron station)
Data Trek (new name: EOS International)	EOS International 5838 Edison Place Carlsbad, CA 92008 (800) 876-5484 (619) 431-8400	Windows, NT, DOS http://www.eosintl.com
Mandarin	SIRS P.O. Box 2348 Boca Raton, Fla. 33427 (800) 232-SIRS (518) 298-2970	DOS, Windows, NT http://www.sirs.com
Molli; Athena	Nichols Advanced Technologies, Inc. 3452 Losey Blvd. South LaCrosse, WI 54601 (800) 658-9453 (608) 787-8333	DOS; Windows and NT (Athena); Webserver Link
Precision One	Brodart Automation 500 Arch St. Williamsport, PA 17705 (800) 233-8467	DOS, Windows (in progress); CD-ROM-based http://www.brodart.com
Unison (Catalog Plus; Circulation Plus)	Follett Software Company 1391 Corporate Dr. McHenry, IL 60050 (800) 323-3397 (815) 344-8700	DOS, Mac, Windows, NT http://www.follett.com
Winnebago	Winnebago Library Software Company 457 E. South St. Caledonia, MN 55921 (800) 533-5430	DOS, Mac, Windows (in progress); Z39.50 (Winnebago Spectrum) http://www.winnebago.com

- The qualifications of the operators performing the Recon. The more skilled the operators are at applying bibliographic standards (i.e., U.S. MARC, *AACR2R,* etc.), the higher the accuracy rate will be. The accuracy rate should not fall below 90 percent.

- The vendor's experience in providing Recon service. (At least five years experience is recommended.)

- The kind of enhancements the vendor is willing to apply to various fields in MARC records as well as the cost of those enhancements.

- The quality of MARC records. Records must be as complete as possible. Media specialists or information professionals should compare samples of MARC records from various vendors before making a final decision on which vendor to use.

- The search parameters used to find matches from shelflist cards (e.g., LCCN, ISBN, title, author–title).

- The provision of authority control, its application to selected fields (e.g., author, subject, series, title), its compatibility with the Library of Congress, and the cost.

- The cost of converting each matched item and manually created record.

- The turnaround time for completing the conversion.

- The vendor's reputation and reliability.

- The clarity of the vendor's guidelines for packing and shipping the shelflist.

In-House Conversion Process

This process requires that a media specialist or information professional or trained staff carry out the conversion. One or more CD-ROM databases of MARC records may be used to support this process. Bibliofile, Precision One, and Alliance Plus are common databases used for this purpose. Manual input of records (i.e., without the use of a MARC database) is not recommended, because it is extremely time-consuming, incurs a high labor cost, and may result in a large number of errors.

To perform Recon in-house, a media specialist or information professional or trained staff searches one or more databases of MARC records to find a match for each item in the shelflist. Searches are performed by LCCN, ISBN, or other standard parameter. The MARC record for each matched item is downloaded onto a diskette. If no match is found for an item in one MARC database, and if the media center or library has access to another database, then the other database may be searched.

Each matched record is paved onto a diskette or the hard drive. Upon completion, matched MARC records are edited and enhanced according to the media center's or library's specifications. Or, editing and enhancements can be done after each match is found or after the MARC records are downloaded into the cataloging database.

A barcode is linked to each matched record. Unmatched items can be created through original cataloging after the cataloging module is implemented.

Diskettes of MARC records should be stored in a safe, secure place. These records will be downloaded into the cataloging module after it is implemented.

Advantages of In-House Conversion

In-house conversion has the following advantages:

- The shelflist remains in the media center or library.

- The media specialist's or information professional's firsthand knowledge of the collection and the shelflist may generate a higher accuracy rate than vendor Recon will.

Disadvantages of In-House Conversion

The disadvantages of in-house conversion outnumber the advantages. Some of the disadvantages are:

- CD-ROM databases may contain fewer MARC records than databases used by a vendor, resulting in a lower match rate. This problem can be remedied by using more than one database—at an additional cost.

- Most CD-ROM databases are updated only monthly or quarterly. This causes a backlog of unmatched items.

- The conversion may take a long time to complete, especially if the media center or library is understaffed. The larger the collection, the longer it will take to complete the conversion.

- Media center or library services, such as user assistance, may be diminished because of staff time devoted to the conversion.

- Constant interruption of staff may result in a high error rate.

- The larger the collection, the greater the cost of labor will be. (See the following cost analysis for a comparison of the costs of vendor and in-house Recon.)

- Any hardware or software failure will delay the conversion.

Combined Conversion Process

This process involves having part of the collection converted by a vendor and part of it converted by media center or library staff. For example, nonprint materials may be converted in-house, and print materials may be sent to a vendor. The same procedures for Recon mentioned earlier are followed. The advantages and disadvantages of this conversion process combine those of both the vendor and in-house conversion.

☐ Cost Analysis for Vendor Versus In-House Recon

Before deciding on a conversion method, perform a cost analysis to determine the most cost-effective and efficient method of conversion. Cost analysis provides justification for choosing a specific method of conversion. A sample cost analysis comparing vendor and in-house conversion is provided here as a guideline. Adapt it to your own situation to estimate and compare the cost of each conversion method.

Cost Analysis for Vendor Conversion

Estimating the cost of vendor conversion should be based on

> the number of items to be converted,
>
> the enhancements that need to be made to the records,
>
> the cost of smart barcodes,
>
> insuring the shelflist for shipping, and
>
> shipping.

Assume that you have a collection of 5,000 items and that the vendor charges $.50 per each item converted and $.05 for each enhancement based on your specifications. The lowest estimated cost would be:

5,000 items @$.50 per item	=	$2,500
5,000 items @$.05 per enhancement	=	$ 250
5,000 items at $.05 per smart barcode linked	=	$ 250
Insurance	=	$ 250
Shipping	=	$ 100
Total	=	$3,600

Cost Analysis for In-House Conversion

Assume that you are considering in-house conversion using a CD-ROM database of MARC records. Your lowest cost estimate should be based on

> cost of subscribing to a CD-ROM database for one year,
>
> cost of subscribing to an additional CD-ROM database for nonprint materials or other materials,
>
> barcode labels, and
>
> labor.

Recon can be performed by a professional or paraprofessional. Because the cost of labor is involved, the cost of the conversion varies by salary. Using a collection size of 5,000 items, the total cost of conversion performed by a professional will range from $8,590 to $21,090, whereas the cost will be about $8,595 when completed by a paraprofessional.

Highest Cost Estimate of Conversion by a Professional

Assume that the collection of 5,000 items is going to be converted by a professional on staff. The highest cost estimate would be:

Salary for 10 months	=	$24,000
Hourly rate = $2,400 per month/160 hours per month	=	$15 per hour
Average number of minutes to convert, edit, and enhance an item	=	15
Number of minutes needed = 5,000 × 15	=	75,000
Number of hours needed = 75,000/60	=	1,250
Labor cost = 1,250 × $15	=	$8,750
Subscription to a CD-ROM database	=	$1,090 per year
Subscription to a CD-ROM database for nonprint materials	=	$1,000 per year
Barcodes	=	$250
Total	=	$21,090

Lowest Cost Estimate of Conversion by a Professional

Suppose that the conversion time per item is reduced from 15 to 5 minutes because of experience. Then, the lowest cost estimate will be:

Salary for ten months	=	$24,000
Hourly rate = $2,400/160 hours per month	=	$15
Average number of minutes to convert, edit, and enhance an item	=	5
Number of minutes needed = 5,000 × 5	=	25,000
Number of hours needed = 25,000/60	=	417
Labor cost = 417 × $15	=	$6,255
Subscription to a CD-ROM database	=	$1,090 per year
Subscription to a CD-ROM database for nonprint materials	=	$1,000 per year
Barcode labels	=	$250
Total	=	$8,590

Cost Estimate of Conversion by a Paraprofessional

To reduce the cost, a paraprofessional may be trained to conduct the conversion. The cost estimate would be:

Hourly rate (salary)	=	$5
Average number of minutes to convert, edit, and enhance an item	=	15
Number of minutes needed = 5,000 × 15	=	75,000
Number of hours needed = 75,000/60	=	1,250
Labor cost = 1,250 × $5	=	$6,250
Subscription to a CD-ROM database	=	$1,090 per year
Subscription to a CD-ROM database for nonprint materials	=	$1,000 per year
Barcode labels	=	$250
Total	=	$8,590

Converting records without the use of a CD-ROM database is not recommended because creating a great number of records is extremely time-consuming and increases both the cost of labor and the number of errors.

■ Bibliographic Standards

The format and content of a database must be based on recognized bibliographic standards (i.e., U.S. MARC, U.S. MARC/MicroLIF Protocol, *AACR2R,* and ISBD). The U.S. MARC standard is used to identify, store, and communicate cataloging information (Crawford 1989). The *AACR2R (Anglo-American Cataloguing Rules, Second Revised Edition*; Gorman and Winkler 1988) consists of a set of rules for describing various types of materials. The ISBD (International Standard Bibliographic Description) provides eight elements to use in describing all types of materials, as well as a system of punctuation among the elements. This book treats only U.S. MARC/MicroLIF Protocol. For information about *AACR2R* and ISBD, refer to the *Concise AACR2R* by Michael Gorman (1989).

Adhering to standards eliminates redundant efforts and thereby reduces cataloging cost, especially in a resource-sharing environment.

□ U.S. MARC

United States Machine-Readable Cataloging (U.S. MARC) was developed by the Library of Congress in late 1960s for use with mainframe computers. The main purpose of the standard is to share automated cataloging among libraries and allow records to be transferred from one automated system to another. A sample U.S. MARC record appears in figure 5.1.

A detailed discussion of U.S. MARC is beyond the scope of this book; for more information on the subject, refer to Furrie (1991 and 1994) and Byrne (1991).

□ U.S. MARC/MicroLIF Protocol

This standard refers to United States Machine-Readable Cataloging Microcomputer Library Interchange Format Protocol. In 1987, a group of book vendors and publishers established MicroLIF, a MARC-based standard for use in microcomputer-based automated systems. Because the standard did not conform with U.S. MARC, it was revised in 1991. The revised standard was named U.S. MARC/MicroLIF Protocol to reflect its full compatibility and conformity with U.S. MARC. When MARC records are requested from book vendors, reference should be made to this protocol.

Note: Knowledge of *AACR2R* is a prerequisite for understanding the MARC record; for more information on the subject, refer to Gorman 1989.

Figure 5.1   A sample U.S. MARC record.

Leader	01041cam		2200265 a 4500
Control #	001		89048230 /AC/r91
Control # Identifier	003	DLC	
DTLT	005	19911106082810.9	
Fixed Data	008	891101s1990 maua j 00110 eng	
LCCN	010	‡ƀƀ	‡a 89048230 /AC/r91
ISBN	020	ƀƀ	‡a 0316107514 :
			‡c $12.95
ISBN	020	ƀƀ	‡a 0316107506 (pbk.) :
			‡c $5.95 ($6.95 Can.)
Cat. Source	040	ƀƀ	‡a DLC
			‡c DLC
			‡d DLC
LC Call No.	050	00	‡a GV943.25
			‡b .B74 1990
Dewey No.	082	00	‡a 796.334/2
			‡2 20
ME: Pers Name	100	1ƀ	‡a Brenner, Richard J.,
			‡d 1941—
Title	245	10	‡a Make the team.
			‡p Soccer :
			‡b a heads up guide to super soccer! /
			‡c Richard J. Brenner.
Edition	250	ƀƀ	‡a 1st ed.
Publication	260	0ƀ	‡a Boston :
			‡b Little, Brown,
			‡c c1990.
Phys Desc	300	ƀƀ	‡a 127 p. :
			‡b ill. ;
			‡c 19 cm.
Note: General	500	ƀƀ	‡a "A Sports illustrated for kids book."
Note: Summary	520	ƀƀ	‡a Instructions for improving soccer skills. Discusses dribbling, heading, playmaking, defense, conditioning, mental attitude, how to handle problems with coaches, parents, and other players, and the history of soccer.
Subj: Topical	650	ƀ0	‡a Soccer
			‡x Juvenile literature.
	650	ƀ1	‡a Soccer.
AE: Dif Titl	740	01	‡a Heads up guide to super soccer.

Understanding MARC Bibliographic, by Betty Furrie. Fourth edition, 1994, published by the Cataloging Distribution Service, Library of Congress, in collaboration with The Follett Software Company.

Components of a U.S. MARC/MicroLIF Protocol Record

The U.S. MARC/MicroLIF Protocol record, like the U.S. MARC record, has various components that describe a cataloged item in an automated system. The difference between the two types of records lies in their format rather than content. A sample U.S. MARC/Micro-LIF Protocol record appears in figure 5.2. Following is a description of the components of a U.S. MARC/MicroLIF Protocol record.

Leader

A Leader (LDR) consists of the first 24 characters that appear in most records. The Leader encodes information that designates the length of a record, the status of a record (e.g., new, deleted, corrected, revised), and the type of record (e.g., book, serial, computer file, kit, sound recording). The Leader must be verified and revised by the cataloger as necessary. An interpretation of the Leader for the item in figure 5.2 is provided below.

000   cam 2200193 a 4500

000	=	Tag.
c	=	This record has been corrected or revised.
a	=	This record is for printed material. (This is the default value.) If this record was for a kit, for example, the value would be **o** instead of **a**.
m	=	This record is for a monograph. If this record was for a periodical, for example, the value would be **s** instead of **m**.
2	=	Indicator count (always set at 2).
2	=	Indicator count for subfield code (always set at 2).
00	=	Base address of data (calculated for each record).
193	=	This record occurs at character 193.
a	=	This record is based on *AACR2R* cataloging. If the record was a CIP cataloging, for example, the value would be **8** instead of **a**.
4	=	Length of the "length-of-field" portion (always 4).
5	=	Length of the "starting-character-position" portion (always 5).
0	=	Length of the "implementation-defined" n portion (always 0).
0	=	Undefined position (always 0).

The main values a cataloger may need to supply (for original cataloging) or verify (for records ordered from vendors) are those relating

Figure 5.2   A sample U.S. MARC/MicroLIF Protocol record.

Leader	000			cam 2200193 a 4500
Control #	001			81047861
Fixed Data	008			810909s1982 nyuaf 00110ceng
LCCN	010		_a	81–047861
ISBN	020		_a	0–385–17771–2
	039		_a	2
			_b	3
			_c	3
			_d	3
			_e	3
Cat. Source	040		_a	DLC
			_c	DLC
			_d	mjhs
	050		_a	Q141
			_b	.A74 1982
	082		_a	509/ .2/2
			_a	B
			_2	19
ME:Pers Name	100	10	_a	Asimov, Isaac,
			_d	1920–1992.
Title	245	10	_a	Asimov's biographical encyclopedia of science and technology :
			_b	the lives and achievements of 1510 great scientists from ancient times to the present chronologically arranged /
			_c	by Isaac Asimov.
Edition	250		_a	2nd rev. ed.
Publication	260		_a	Garden City, N.Y. :
			_b	Doubleday,
			_c	1982.
Phys Desc	300		_a	xxxv, 941 p., [24] p. of plates :
			_b	ill. ;
			_c	24 cm.
Note: General	500		_a	Includes index.
	510	3ø	_a	Junior High School Library Catalog (Wilson)
	510	3ø	_a	Booklist
Note: Summary	520		_a	Compiles chronologically, from ancient times to the present, short biographies of 1510 scientists.
	521	0ø	_a	9.6
	521	2ø	_a	6–8
Sub:Topical	650	0	_a	Scientists
			_x	Biography.
	650	8	_a	Scientists
			_x	Biography.
AE:Dif ttl	740	01	_a	Biographical encyclopedia of science and technology.
Local Call#	900		_a	REF 920'ASI

In this figure, the first column gives the field name, the second column is the tag, the third column is the indicator (as applicable), the fourth column is the subfield code preceded by a delimiter, and the fifth column is the cataloging information.

to the general type of the item cataloged (print or nonprint), record status (e.g., new, corrected, revised), and the kind of item cataloged (e.g., monograph, kit, computer file). Most automated systems supply the rest of the information automatically. This is done after the automated system is implemented. It is not done on paper; it is performed in the cataloging module after the automation software has been installed and tested for proper operation. Some automation software packages, such as Unison, allow the cataloger to select the type of material being cataloged from a menu, then the software itself supplies all the values for the Leader.

Fixed Field (Tag 008)

The term *fixed field* is widely used to refer to the MARC tag 008. (Note: Tags are defined on page 98.) It describes the work cataloged (e.g., book, serial, software; its language; other details) and manages information retrieval by limiting results to material type, grade level, publication date, and other parameters. The field is called a fixed field because it embraces codes (i.e., letters and numbers) rather than textual information and because it does not vary in length. Codes in this field vary from one cataloged item to another. An interpretation of the fixed field for the item in figure 5.2 is provided below.

Fixed Data 008 810909s1982 nyuaf 00110ceng

008	=	Tag for the fixed field.
81	=	CIP cataloging was created in 1981.
0909	=	The record was entered on September 9.
s	=	The item has a single publication date.
1982	=	The item was published in 1982.
nyu	=	Where the item was published (in this case, New York, United States).
a	=	The item has illustrations.
f	=	The item has plates.
00110	=	The first 0 means the item is not a conference publication, the second 0 means the item is not a festschrift, the first number 1 means the item has an index, the second number 1 means the item has a main entry, and the last 0 means the item is not fiction.
c	=	The item is a collective biography.
eng	=	The item is in the English language.

These values (codes) change based on the item being cataloged. If not present in a record, they need to be supplied by the cataloger. A good source for finding these codes is Yurczyk (1995).

Variable Fields

There are two types of variable fields: variable control fields and variable data fields.

Variable Control Fields (001–009). Variable control fields include tags 001 (control number), 005 (date and time of last transaction), 007 (physical description fixed field, i.e., physical characteristics of an item in code form), 008 (fixed field), and 009 (local use field). These fields do not have indicators or subfield codes and contain information expressed through the use of codes. (Indicators and subfield codes are defined later in this section.)

Variable Data Fields (Tags 010–900). Variable data fields include tags 010 (Library of Congress control number); 020 (International Standard Book Number); 022 (International Standard Serial Number); 040 (cataloging source); 041 (language code); 050 (Library of Congress call number); 092 (Dewey Decimal call number); 090 (local call numbers, which has been substituted by tag 900); and tags 100s to 900 (Follett Software Company 1995; Byrne 1991). Variable data fields contain information expressed in text rather than code. They are called variable data fields because they vary in length and they contain indicators and subfield codes. (Indicators and subfield codes are defined later in this section.)

Local Field (Tag 900)

The local field, indicated by tag 900, is reserved for local information (e.g., call number, barcode number, vendor information, price). In figure 5.2, the local field (the last line in figure 5.2) contains the call number assigned to the reference encyclopedia by Asimov: REF 920′ ASI.

Tags

Each variable field in a record (e.g., author, title, series) is identified by a three-digit code called a tag. The tag tells the computer what kind of information is contained in a particular field. Tag 100, for example, is reserved for an item's personal author main entry; tag 245 is reserved for its title and statement of responsibility.

Figure 5.3 lists general tags and field names in the hundreds series, and figure 5.4 lists the most frequently used tags.

Figure 5.3   **General tags and field names in the hundreds.**

Tag	Field Name
0XX	Variable control fields
1XX*	Main entry
2XX	Titles and statement of responsibility
3XX	Physical description
4XX*	Series statement
5XX	Notes
6XX*	Subject added entries
7XX*	Author or title added entries
8XX*	Series added entries
9XX	Local field (e.g., local call number, vendor information, bar code number, price)

*These fields require authority control.

Figure 5.4   **Most frequently-used tags in a U.S. MARC/MicroLIF Protocol record.**

010	LCCN
020	ISBN
100	Personal name main entry
245	Title and statement of responsibility
250	Edition (or version number for a computer file, a map's scale, etc., as applicable)
260	Publication information
300	Physical description
440	Series
500	Notes (e.g., general note, index, references)
520	Annotation, summary, etc.
650	Topical subject headings
700	Personal name added entry
800	Series added entry
900	Local field (e.g., local call number, vendor information, bar code number, price)

Indicators

Associated with each tag are two positions (or digits) reserved to further describe the contents of the field. For example, in the name field, the name may be just a first name, just a family name, or the standard first and last name and the indicators relate to the formats of these entries. Indicators apply to tags 100s 200s, 400s, 500s, 600s, 700s, and 800s. Indicators appear as Arabic numerals next to a field tag.

Indicators vary from one field to another, according to the rules of U.S. MARC/MicroLIF Protocol. For example, indicators in the personal name main entry field (tag 100) vary with the type of name:

   0 for forename. Example: Cher.

  10 for single surname. Example: Asimov, Isaac.

  20 for multiple surname. Example: De Mornay, Rebecca.

  20 for hyphenated surname. Example: Louis-Dreyfuss, Julia.

  30 for family name. Example: The Bensons.

Indicators in the title field (tag 245) vary depending on whether

- An item has a main entry in tag 100
- An item does not have a main entry in tag 100
- An item begins with an initial article
- An item does not begin with an initial article

An item has a main entry in tag 100. When an item has a main entry in tag 100, the first indicator digit in tag 245 is 1. This indicates to the computer that a title added entry is needed.

Tag	Indicator	Title
100	10	
245	14	The librarian and reference queries

An item does not have a main entry in tag 100. When an item does not have a main entry in tag 100, the first indicator digit is zero (0) because the title becomes the main entry (based on *AACR2R*).

Tag	Indicator	Title
245	0	Library research made easy

An item begins with an initial article. When the title of an item begins with an initial article, the second indicator digit indicates the number of characters in the initial article (e.g., a, an, the) *plus* a single space. This tells the computer to ignore the article (plus one space) when filing a record by title. As illustrated in the previous examples, four characters must be ignored in filing *The librarian and reference queries*—three characters for the word *The* and one for the space following it.

An item does not begin with an initial article. When the title of an item does not begin with an initial article *and* it has a main entry in tag 100, the second indicator digit is a zero (0), because there are no characters to be ignored in filing the record by title.

Tag	Indicator	Title
100	10	Asimov, Isaac.
245	10	Asimov's biographical encyclopedia of science and technology:

Indicators must also be applied to author added entries (tags 700s), and series (tags 800s). To find these indicators, use one of the MARC guides listed at the end of this chapter.

Subfield Codes

Each field may be divided into subfields. A field may have one, two, three, or more subfields. The value of a field varies within its subfields and from one field to another. The publication field (tag 260), for example, contains three subfields; they indicate place of publication, publisher, and publication date and bear the values a, b, and c, respectively. The following example is pulled from figure 5.2:

Tag	Delimiter and subfield code	Content of Field
260	_a	Garden City, N.Y.:
	_b	Doubleday,
	_c	1982/

Delimiters. Each subfield code is preceded by a special symbol called a delimiter. (In the preceding example, the delimiter is _.) A delimiter varies from one MARC record to another, depending on the automated system in place. A delimiter may appear as a double dagger (‡), a dollar sign ($), an underscore (_), or another form. Whatever its form, the delimiter appears before each subfield code.

Because tags, indicators, and subfield codes identify each element in a bibliographic record, they are known as **content designators**. Values for all components of a MARC record can be found in a MARC manual.

☐ *Anglo-American Cataloguing Rules, Second Revised Edition (AACR2R)*

Anglo-American Cataloguing Rules are based on a set of standard rules for describing various types of materials. Published in 1967, the rules were revised in 1978 "to bring together the separate North American and British texts of 1967 . . . and to reorganize and express the rules in a simpler and more direct way" (Gorman 1989, p. vii). The rules were revised again in 1988; at that time they became known as *AACR2R* (Gorman and Winkler 1988). Adherence to the rules is important for maintaining consistency in cataloging and for providing effective information retrieval.

☐ International Standard Bibliographic Description (ISBD)

ISBD is a standard that provides eight elements of description for various types of materials and a system of punctuation among the elements. The elements, called areas, are

> Title and Statement of Responsibility Area
>
> Edition Area
>
> Special area for serials, computer files, maps and other cartographic materials, and Music Area
>
> Publication, Distribution, etc., Area
>
> Physical Description Area
>
> Series Area
>
> Note Area
>
> Standard Number

■ Barcoding the Collection

Barcoding is the process of placing a barcode on each item in the database. A barcode identifies a specific item and allows it to be checked in and out by using a barcode scanner or by keying in the barcode number to enter it into the automated system.

Figure 5.5   **Code 39 Mod 10 barcode.**

Used with permission of Follett Software Company, McHenry, IL.

□ Barcodes

A barcode contains both bars and spaces. A row of numbers (up to 14 digits) appears under the code to indicate the meaning of the bars and spaces (Follett Software Company 1994).

There are two main barcode standards: Codabar and Code 39. Within these standards, there are various types of barcodes, for example, in Code 39 are the types Mod 10, Mod 11, and Mod 43. As seen in figure 5.5, a Code 39 Mod 10 barcode has four components: type indicator or barcode type (e.g., patron, item); location code; identification number (e.g., of an item or patron); and a check digit, which verifies the accuracy of the barcode during scanning. Patron barcodes must be distinguished from material barcodes. Barcodes that start with number 1 may be assigned to patrons, for example, and those that begin with number 2 may be assigned to materials. Barcodes must be compatible with the automated system in place, regardless of the standard or type used.

Type of Barcodes: Smart and Dumb

There are two types of barcodes, smart barcodes and dumb barcodes. Smart barcodes are linked to their respective items during Recon. A smart barcode identifies its respective item without scanning it in the automated system because it contains the item's title, call number, and author. Dumb barcodes are generic; they do not identify any items until they are linked to their respective items in the automated system. When purchased, dumb barcodes may contain the name of the media center or library, but because they are not linked to any items, they do not identify an item's call number, title, or author. Linking dumb barcodes to their respective items may be performed as materials are cataloged, converted, or during check-out.

Acquiring Barcodes

Barcodes are acquired through a vendor or are generated in-house using barcode production software that is compatible with the existing automated system. Few automated systems have barcode generator software. Before making a decision to purchase barcodes or generate them in-house, perform a cost analysis to determine the most cost-effective method.

Barcodes must be compatible with the automated system in place. Before ordering barcodes, develop specifications for them. You may specify that each smart barcode should include the name of the media center or library; the item's title, call number, and author; and other information you determine is useful.

Keep the barcode range on file so that each time additional barcodes are ordered, the barcodes are kept in correct sequence.

During barcoding, you may encounter errors in barcode labels (e.g., in call numbers or titles) and find that several barcodes are missing. If these or other problems occur, contact the vendor for replacement. If this problem is detected for barcodes generated in-house, then the barcodes will need to be re-generated.

Generating Barcodes In-House

Some barcode production software packages include Laser Barcode Production software, from Winnebago Library Software Company, and Print Pack and Label Pro, from Nichols Advanced Technologies, Inc.

The Laser Barcode Production software is compatible with the Winnebago automated system. The cost, at this writing, is $200. Laser labels and a Hewlett Packard laser jet printer are required to support the software. The cost of labels at this writing is $19.95 for 3,300 labels. The cost of the printer ranges from $400 to $800 (Winnebago Library Software Company 1996).

The Print Pack software is compatible with the Molli automated system. It prints several types of labels and barcodes, including regular barcodes, barcodes for library cards, videotape labels, and mailing labels for overdues or other purposes. The cost of the software at this writing is $195 for use with either a dot matrix or laser printer and $295 for use with both.

The Label Pro software works with the Athena automated system, the Windows version of Molli. It prints barcodes only and requires a laser printer. The cost of the software at this writing is $89 for use with either a laser or dot matrix printer (Nichols Advanced Technologies 1996).

☐ Procedures for Barcoding the Collection

Barcoding is a very time-consuming process. The larger the collection, the more time it will take to barcode it. The availability of adequate staffing and the development of a good barcoding plan may reduce barcoding time. For example, before barcoding begins, it must be determined which materials will be barcoded. For example, Will materials in the vertical file be barcoded?

Following are procedures that may facilitate barcoding.

- Make an effort to close the media center or library to the public to avoid interruption and to expedite the process.

- Recall checked-out items.

- Divide the shelves into sections, and barcode one section at a time. If adequate staffing is available, one or more staff members may be given responsibility for barcoding one or more sections.

- Use the smart barcodes first, because they are arranged by call numbers and, possibly, by categories (e.g., fiction, biographies). (A media center or library would have smart barcodes for items converted by the vendor and dumb barcodes for items cataloged after the conversion was completed.)

- Verify each item's call number against the call number on the barcode. If they match, place the barcode on the item in the designated area. Make sure all smart barcodes have respective items in the collection.

Protecting Barcodes

Scanning barcodes causes them to deteriorate over time unless they are laminated or covered with protectors. In addition, barcodes are subject to vandalism. Make sure that barcodes are safeguarded against both types of damage. If the barcode labels have good protectors, then users will find them hard to remove.

Placing Barcodes on Print Materials

Where on the item a barcode is placed is determined by how items are scanned during inventory and by the type of material (e.g., print, audio disc, videotape) being barcoded. To choose the best placement, first simulate the collection inventory process by selecting sample items to scan. Determine the barcode placement that will make scanning easiest and fastest.

There are many options for barcoding print materials. Following are some of the options:

Place the barcode on the front book cover in the top right or top left corner, vertically or horizontally.

Place the barcode on the outside of the back cover in the top right or top left corner, vertically or horizontally.

Place the barcode inside the back cover in the top right or top left corner, vertically or horizontally.

Place the barcode inside the front cover in the top right or top left corner, vertically or horizontally.

Place two identical barcodes, one inside and one outside the cover in the top right or top left corner, vertically or horizontally.

Avoid placing a barcode on an item's spine or where any information will be covered.

Barcoding Electronic Materials

Barcoding electronic materials, such as CD-ROMs, audio tapes, videocassettes, audio disks, laserdiscs, and computer software requires careful consideration, because barcode scanning may damage the encoded information.

Most electronic materials are multipart items because they include accompanying pieces (e.g., guides, manuals, booklets). Recommendations for barcoding these materials are listed below.

Place a barcode on the outside of an item's container, cover, or jacket, preferably in the upper left corner.

Transcribe the barcode number on each accompanying piece (e.g., booklet, guide) using a permanent marker.

Label each accompanying item above or below the barcode number to alert circulation staff that the item is part of a set.

Transcribe the barcode number on the item's label using a permanent marker.

■ Summary

Collection preparation is the first step in implementing the automation project. Many decisions need to be made at this stage, especially with regard to weeding the collection, identifying the part of collection that is the subject for Recon, the method of Recon to embrace, the Recon vendor to choose, and the kind of Recon specifications to adopt.

Regardless of the method of Recon you choose (e.g., vendor, in-house, or a combination of both), it is important that you develop specifications. Developing specifications, however, requires adequate knowledge of the various components of a MARC record format. Knowledge of *AACR2R* is a prerequisite for understanding the MARC record, for detecting errors in cataloging, and for maintaining consistency in the content of the MARC database. This chapter briefly covers the components of a MARC/MicroLIF Protocol record.

Preparing the collection also requires barcoding it so that it can be checked out, checked in, and inventoried using an inventory device. Barcoding the collection is recommended after testing and installation of the automated system, because conversion vendors supply the smart barcodes after coverting the shelflist into a MARC format. Before barcoding the collection, make a decision about barcode placement on print and nonprint materials. Performing these collection activities should prepare you to undertake the next steps in system implementation (i.e., site preparation, software installation and testing, user training, and database management), which are described in chapter 6.

■ References

Byrne, Deborah J. 1991. *MARC manual: Understanding and using MARC records*. Englewood, CO: Libraries Unlimited.

Crawford, Walt. 1989. *MARC for library use*. Boston, MA: G. K. Hall.

Follett Software Company. 1994. *Utilities reference guide for the Follett Unison platform*. McHenry, IL: Follett Software Company.

Furrie, Betty. 1994. *Understanding MARC (machine-readable cataloging)*. Washington, DC: Library of Congress.

———. 1991. *Understanding MARC (machine-readable cataloging)*. McHenry, IL: Follett Software Company.

Gorman, Michael. 1989. *The concise AACR2R: 1988 revision*. Chicago: American Library Association.

Gorman, Michael, and Paul Winkler. 1988. *Anglo-American Cataloguing Rules, Second Revised Edition*. Chicago: American Library Association.

Nichols Advanced Technologies. 1996. *Library automation catalog*. LaCrosse, WI: Nichols Advanced Technologies.

Winnebago Library Software Company. 1996. *1995/1996 catalog*. Caledonia, MN: Winnebago Library Software Company.

Yurczyk, Judith. 1995. *MARC bibliographic format guide*. McHenry, IL: Follett Software Company.

Activity: Cost Analysis for Recon

Objective: To perform a cost analysis for Recon of a specific media center or small library collection.

Description: 1. Select a media center or a small library that is preparing for automation.

2. Determine the method of conversion (i.e., vendor, in-house, or combined) the media specialist or information professional is planning to adopt.

3. Determine the size of the collection, including print and nonprint materials.

4. Contact a few Recon vendors to determine the cost to convert each item, including the cost of enhancing items.

5. Call suppliers to determine the cost of subscribing to or leasing a CD-ROM database of MARC records for one year.

6. Calculate the estimated cost of both vendor and in-house conversion using the cost analysis methods provided in this chapter.

7. Describe which method you would adopt and state the reasons why.

6 Implementing the Automated System

■ Site Preparation

If the new automated system will run on existing hardware, then a completely new computer facility need not be designed, but the location and arrangement of the existing computers may need to be rethought. When existing hardware is not already in place, planning the selection and placement of computer stations, printers, barcode scanners, furniture, and other equipment must be done in advance so that necessary hardware is available during system installation and testing.

□ Selection and Placement of Hardware

Computer Stations

Two types of computer stations are needed for automated systems: look-up stations and administrative stations. The number of stations to acquire depends on an estimate of the number of users who will access OPAC simultaneously and on the number of employees who will be assisting users and performing administrative tasks. One should also take into consideration whether the building where the media center or library is located is or will be wired to support a local area network (LAN). In a networked environment, access to OPAC may be available from offices, computer laboratories, or other locations.

One look-up station is recommended for every 50–100 users. At least one computer station is needed to support circulation and information services functions, and another computer station is needed for administrative tasks (e.g., preparing statistics reports, overdue notices). The kind of look-up stations is based on the specifications recommended by the software vendor and specified in your RFP for hardware.

Computer stations must be compatible with the automation software. For this reason, they must meet the specifications established by software vendors. Adherence to vendors' specifications is highly recommended to ensure proper operation of the automated system.

Look-up stations may be scattered throughout the media center or library or may be clustered in one or more locations to resemble a computer laboratory or study area. Stations should be placed close to staff to ensure that user assistance is readily available and to monitor system security. Also, in placing stations, take into account direct sunlight, heat or drafts, glare from windows, traffic patterns, and existing electrical wiring.

Hardware, computer stations, the file server or host computer, and the hubs and other hardware devices supporting the operation of the LAN should be located in a cool, clean, and secure area. The cabling system connecting the LAN should be covered with conduits to protect users from tripping over them and to avoid loss of data that could occur if the cables were inadvertently disconnected. The endpoint of the LAN cabling system and the hubs should be placed in a secure wiring closet away from users. Cables, wires, and computer stations should be isolated from moisture, mold, and water. Areas that are susceptible to flood (e.g., a basement) should not be considered for storing the LAN wiring closet, hubs, or other devices supporting the LAN.

Printers

Printers allow OPAC users to generate bibliographies and to print citations. They are also used to support administrative tasks. One printer is recommended for every five look-up stations. Another printer will be needed to support administrative tasks. Dot matrix or other low-end printers may be used for look-up stations, and ink jet or laser printers for administrative stations. The purchase of printers should be based on the recommendation of the software vendor and should be specified in your RFP for hardware.

☐ Selection of Furniture

Computer stations are usually placed on tables of various heights so that users may either sit or stand while using them. When purchasing furniture, pay attention to all users, including those with special needs. Furniture, especially chairs, should be ergonomic and comfortable. Wright (1995) describes the ergonomic issues and health concerns involved in site and facility design for automation. For more information, refer to Wright and other sources listed at the end of this chapter.

■ Installation and Testing

After retrospective conversion is completed and hardware and software are available, the automation software is installed and tested. Many problems may occur during and after installation. Failure to access one or more modules (such as the cataloging module or the circulation module) is one possible problem. Other problems may involve the use of peripherals, such as barcode scanners and printers. Testing the system thoroughly, including the use of all peripherals in all modules, is essential to ensure the proper operation of the system, its software and hardware compatibility, and its conformity to the needs and requirements (or specifications) of the media center or library.

The automated system must not become available for use before all problems are worked out and staff are trained and proficient in using it. To become acquainted with the automated system during the testing period, catalog a few titles, enter selected patron records, circulate a few items, prepare purchase orders (in the acquisitions module), customize selected features (in the utilities module), and retrieve selected titles (in the OPAC module). Allow a minimum of one week for you and your staff to become familiar with the system.

□ Building the Database of Patron Records

Creating patron records in the circulation module is time-consuming. Staff, students, and other clients must have circulation records containing their name, address, telephone number, social security number, home room number (for public schools), and other necessary information.

Many public schools have software for student record management. If that software is compatible with the automated system, the student records can be downloaded from the record management software to the automated system. This will save a tremendous amount of time that would otherwise be spent creating student records manually.

■ Security

Computer systems are vulnerable to breaches by computer hackers. Hackers may modify or destroy local files, inflict viruses, and break into remote systems. Although password protection is inherent in many automated systems' software, hackers can install password sniffers to encrypt and capture passwords over a network (Daly 1994). Therefore, media centers and libraries must adopt security measures to protect the software and hardware from serious harm. Measures may include installing antivirus and security software on all computer stations, scanning users' floppy disks for viruses before allowing them to be used in the system, and using locking devices on computer stations to prevent theft. Ives (1996) provides strategies for protecting your library's network. Table 6.1 lists selected vendors of security systems and devices. For evaluations of library security systems and

Table 6.1 Selected Vendors of Security Systems and Devices

Company	Address	Internet Address
Brodart Library Supplies	1609 Memorial Ave. Williamsport, PA 17701 (800) 233-8959	http://www.brodard.com
Checkpoint Systems	101 Wolf Dr. Thorofare, NJ 08086 (800) 257-5540	http://www.checkpointsystems.com
Computer Security Products, Inc.	P.O. Box 7544 Nashua, NH 03060 (800) 466-7636	http://www.ComputerSecurity.com
Gaylord Library Supplies	P.O. Box 4901 Syracuse, NY 13221 (800) 448-6160	http://www.gaylord.com
Highsmith Company	P.O. Box 800 Fort Atkinson, WI 53538 (800) 558-2110	http://www.hpress.highsmith.com
Innovative Security	P.O. Box 8682 Prairie Village, KS 66208 (913) 385-2002	http://www.isecure.com
SOLINET	1438 W. Peachtree St. Suite 200 N.W. Atlanta, GA 30309 (800) 999-8558	http://www.solinet.net
Sudanco	3217 Crites Fort Worth, TX 76118 (800) 275-2824	http://www.sudanco.com
3M Innovation Network	P.O. Box 33682 St. Paul, MN 55133 (800) 364-3577	http://www.mmm.com/library

devices, consult *Library Technology Reports. PC Magazine* also evaluates various types of hardware.

Safeguards must also be taken to prevent book theft. Like computer hackers, book thieves can find ways to override a security system to sneak books out of the facility or to smuggle books from areas that are not protected by an alarm. Book theft is a problem facing all libraries, including the Library of Congress, which lost 300,000 books from its collection in 1992 (St. Lifer 1994).

Installing a security system is a good preventive measure against theft of materials. To increase security, however, security personnel may need to monitor the media center or library facility on a regular basis to prevent theft, vandalism, and other problems.

■ OPAC and User Instruction

Information retrieval skills have become vital. "There is no longer any question that knowing how to seek information electronically will be an essential skill for all individuals" (Aversa and Mancall 1989). On-line catalogs have revolutionized the way users access information; the power of OPACs to search by author, title, subject, keyword, and Boolean logic far exceed the search strategies that can be used with the card catalog (Meghabghab 1994). Although OPACs have solved many information access problems inherent in card catalogs (e.g., knowledge of filing rules, alphabetization, and lack of keyword access), they created new ones, especially in relation to subject access and Boolean searching.

Both adults and children have experienced problems in using OPACs. Inability to formulate appropriate search strategies; inadequate use of Boolean operators; uncertainty, frustration, confusion, lack of focus; and difficulties in managing search results are at the heart of these problems (Walter, Borgman, and Hirsch 1996; Solomon 1993; Chen 1993; Wallace 1993; Ensor 1992; Kuhlthau 1991; Edmonds, Moore, and Balcom 1990; Blazek and Bilal 1988).

The difficulties users encounter as they use OPACs have serious implications for library instruction. Media specialists and information professionals should develop effective library instruction programs to train users in information retrieval. Training should be provided based on users' assessment of their own information-seeking behavior and their successes and failures in using OPACs. Programs may teach construction of a search strategy, query formulation and reformulation, keyword selection, hierarchical structure of concepts (i.e., broader terms, narrower terms, and related terms), selection of concepts, term associations, structure and content of citations, effective use of Boolean operators, and management and evaluation of search results. Although poor system design contributes to users' difficulties, it is only through effective instructional programs that deficiencies in information retrieval skills can be remedied, regardless of the OPAC used.

■ Database Management

Database management is the process of maintaining a database to reflect the status of items (e.g., existing, missing, lost, withdrawn). In an integrated microcomputer-based automated system records to be maintained include patron records in the circulation module, bibliographic records in the cataloging module, material orders in the acquisitions module, and serials records in the ʿserials module. While maintaining record accuracy in every module is important, the cataloging module that stores MARC records should be given top priority, because it directly affects the ability of users to retrieve information. This section focuses on the process of cleaning up and purifying MARC records.

□ Why Maintain the Database?

Maintenance should be performed for MARC records on a regular basis to ensure

consistency with *AACR2R* application;

the completeness and accuracy in each record's Leader;

the completeness and accuracy in each record's fixed field (tag 008);

the accuracy of MARC indicators in the main entry fields (tag 100s);

the accuracy of MARC indicators in the title field (tag 245);

the accuracy of MARC indicators in the series field (tag 400s);

the accuracy of MARC indicators in added entry fields (tags 700s and tag 800);

the absence of duplicate entries in author and subject headings fields; and

the accuracy of record filing in author, title, and subject fields.

Database maintenance is essential, whether the original conversion was done in-house or by a vendor. During the conversion, many errors and inaccuracies may have been committed, including mismatched records, incorrect indicators, incomplete fields, missing fields, inconsistent punctuation, and typographical errors. All of these errors and inconsistencies warrant database maintenance.

To keep up with error correction, create a box and label it Corrections. As you encounter errors in the database, print out the records requiring correction and place them in the box. Correct the errors as time allows.

Database maintenance may involve the Leader; fixed field; author fields; title field; subject fields; and alphabetical filing of author, title, and subject entries.

□ The Leader (Tag 007)

The main codes to examine in the Leader are those that pertain to the general type of material cataloged (i.e., print versus nonprint material) and the specific type of material (i.e., monograph, kit, computer file, printed music, projected medium, and so forth). The accuracy of these codes is essential for limiting searches in OPAC by material type and for generating printed lists of various types of materials. The latter may be used to present a statistical comparison of materials for the benefit of balancing the collection.

To maintain the Leader:

1. Examine tag 007 in MARC records.

2. Consult a MARC manual for the correct codes.

3. Make the necessary changes.

4. Save the records.

☐ Fixed Field (Tag 008)

The data elements in the fixed field (tag 008) are frequently overlooked by media specialists and information professionals. Codes in this field may be used to limit searches in OPAC by publication date, country name, audience level, language, and other characteristics.

To detect errors in the fixed field:

1. Complete the date of publication of an item bearing the default value 19uu. If an item is published in 1995, for example, the 19uu should be changed to 1995.

2. Keep the default value **s**, indicating a single date, if an item has only one of the following: publication date or copyright date that are identified.

3. Modify the symbol **s** to **m** if an item bears both a publication date and a copyright date, if they differ.

4. Enter the date of publication first in the default value 19uu, followed by the copyright date. (The publication or copyright date in the fixed field must be based on the date that appears in tag 260 of an item's MARC record.)

5. Modify the default value (nyu), if it exists, to include the state and country of publication of the item.

6. Modify additional default values concerning illustrations, target audience, fiction, biography, and language, as applicable.

☐ Author Fields (Tag 100s)

An example of an author field is tag 100, which is reserved for a personal author main entry. There are two elements to consider in this tag—the correct entry of an author name (i.e., for hyphenated and

Table 6.2 **Indicators in the Author Field (Tag 100)**

Type of Personal Name	Example	Indicator (Tag 100)
Forename only	Cher.	0
Forename and surname	Blume, Judy.	10
	Maupassant, Guy de.	10
Surname and a word	Seuss, Dr.	10
Multiple surname	De Mornay, Rebecca.	20
Hyphenated surname	Williams-Ellis, Annabel	20
Family name	The Kennedys	30

multiple surnames) and the indicator. The indicator instructs the system about how to file a name in correct alphabetical order. Various indicators for this field are shown in table 6.2.

To detect errors in this field:

1. Browse OPAC by author under various letters.

2. Examine the alphabetization for correctness.

3. Transcribe or print out the entries for the records containing errors.

4. Exit OPAC.

5. Search the cataloging module under each entry that needs to be corrected.

6. Examine both the correct form of an author entry and its indicator.

7. Make the necessary corrections.

8. Save the record.

9. Go back to OPAC and look up the corrected records to verify their accuracy.

Another area to consider in main entry fields is the elimination of duplicate entries for identical names. An entry that ends with a period and an identical one that does not end with a period will appear as two separate entries in OPAC. Duplication will occupy disk space and cause confusion for the user. Based on *AACR2R,* all types of main entries (in tag 100s) must end with a period.

To detect errors in this field:

1. Browse a sample of author entries in OPAC.

2. Transcribe or print out the entries needing correction.

Table 6.3 Indicators in the Title Field (Tag 245)

Main Entry (Tag 100)	Title (Tag 245)	Initial article	Added entry	Indicator
Carroll, Lewis.	The hunting of the snark	The	Yes	14
Hugo, Victor.	Les miserables	Les	Yes	14
None	The ALA glossary of library	The	No	04
Bigham, Dane.	Where in the world is Carmen	None	Yes	10
Boyer, Carl B.	A history of mathematics and	A	Yes	12

3. Exit OPAC.

4. Correct the entries in the cataloging module. Use the global editing feature, if available; otherwise, correct each record individually.

5. Save the changes.

6. Go back to OPAC and look up the entries to verify their accuracy.

□ Title Field (Tag 245)

The indicator associated with the title field (tag 245) does two things: It indicates to the automated system whether to make the title an added entry, and it instructs the computer about how to file a title. Various indicators applicable to this field are listed in table 6.3.

If your automated system maintains a list of stop words or initial articles and automatically ignores nonfiling characters, you will need to apply the correct indicator to the first digit only. Errors occur in filing records by title when the indicators in tag 245 are incorrect.

To detect errors in this field:

1. Browse OPAC by title under various letters.

2. Examine the alphabetization for correctness.

3. Transcribe or print out the entries for the records containing errors.

4. Exit OPAC.

5. Search the cataloging module under each entry that needs to be corrected.

6. Examine the number of characters of the initial articles in the title and the indicator in the title field.

7. Make the necessary corrections.

8.   Save the record.

9.   Go back to OPAC and look up the corrected records to verify their accuracy.

☐ Subject Headings Fields (Tag 600s)

The main problems relating to this field involve duplicate entries for identical subject headings. This problem occurs when imported MARC records contain identical *Sears* and LC subject headings. Duplication also occurs when one heading ends with a period and its identical one does not.

To detect duplicate entries in this field:

1.   Browse OPAC by subject under various letters.

2.   Examine the subject headings for correct endings (i.e., with a period).

3.   Transcribe or print out the subject headings for the records where there is no period at the end of each subject heading.

4.   Exit OPAC.

5.   Search the cataloging module under each subject heading. Use the global editing feature, if available, to add a period to the end of each heading. The automated system should merge identical headings after the correction. (This means that identical LC and *Sears* headings will appear once instead of twice in OPAC, while maintaining their presence in the cataloging module. You may also delete LC headings and keep *Sears* headings, or vice versa.)

6.   Save the changes.

7.   Go back to OPAC and look up the records to verify their accuracy.

☐ Added Entry Fields (Tags 700s–800s)

Indicators for tag 700 (personal name added entry), 710 (corporate name added entry), 740 (related or variant title added entry), 800 (personal name series added entry), and 830 (uniform title series added entry) require verification. Adapt the aforementioned methods to detect errors in these fields. Consult a MARC manual for the appropriate indicators.

■ Summary

The media center's or library's physical layout may need to be redesigned for efficiently placing computer stations, printers, furniture, and other equipment. Both look-up stations and computers for administrative use must be procured. All hardware must adhere to the software vendor's specifications to ensure proper operation of the automated system. Lookup stations should be placed in proximity to staff so that user assistance is readily available and software and hardware can be observed for security.

Software installation should be followed by a thorough testing of the automated system to ensure hardware and software compatibility and the system's conformity to the media center's or library's specifications.

Computer systems are vulnerable to theft and breaches by computer hackers. Safeguard measures must be taken to prevent unauthorized use, virus infliction, theft, and other problems that may occur.

User training is highly recommended after system implementation. Research has revealed that both adults and children experience problems in using OPACs. Therefore, effective library instruction programs should be developed to train users in information retrieval skills.

Database maintenance should be performed on a regular basis to provide consistency and accuracy in the content of MARC records and to reflect the accurate status of the collection. Maintenance in the cataloging module should comprise various fields to include the Leader, fixed field, author, title, subjects, and added entries. Maintenance should also comprise purging MARC records for items withdrawn from the collection.

■ References

Anthes, Gary H. 1996. Hackers set up attacks. *Computer World* 30 (June): 65.

Aversa, Elizabeth S., and Jacqueline C. Mancall. 1989. *Management of online search services in schools.* Santa Barbara, CA: ABC-CLIO.

Blazek, Ron, and Dania Bilal. 1988. Problems in OPAC: A case of an academic research library. *RQ* 28 (Winter): 169–78.

Byrne, Deborah J. 1991. *MARC manual: Understanding and using MARC records.* Englewood, CO: Libraries Unlimited.

Chen, Shu-Hsien. 1993. A study of high school students' online catalog searching behavior. *School Library Media Quarterly* 22 (Fall): 33–40.

Daly, James. 1994. Breaking and entering. *Computer World* 28 (March): 53.

Delaney, Tom. 1996. "If you think your system hasn't been compromised, think again." *Computers in Libraries* 16 (February): 8.

Edmonds, Leslie, Paula Moore, and Kathleen Mehaffey Balcom. 1990. The effectiveness of an online catalog. *School Library Journal* 36 (October): 28–33.

Ensor, Pat. 1992. Knowledge level of users and nonusers of keyword and Boolean searching on an online public access catalog. *RQ* 32 (Fall): 60–74.

Furrie, Betty. 1994. *Understanding MARC (machine-readable cataloging) bibliographic.* Washington, DC : Library of Congress.

———. 1991. *Understanding MARC (machine-readable cataloging).* McHenry, IL : Follett Software Company.

Ives, David J. 1996. Security management strategies for protecting your library's network. *Computers in Libraries.* 16 (February): 38–42.

Knoblauch, Carol, and Judy Parr. 1994. *Planning for library automation: A how-to guide for librarians.* Dublin, OH: Information Dimensions.

Kuhlthau, Carol C. 1991. Inside the search process: Information seeking from the user's perspective. *Journal of the American Society for Information Science* 42 (5): 361–71.

Solomon, Paul. 1993. Children's information retrieval behavior: A case analysis of an OPAC. *Journal of the American Society for Information Science* 44 (5): 245–64.

St. Lifer, Evan. 1994. How safe are our libraries? *Library Journal* 119 (August): 35–39.

Wallace, Patricia M. 1993. How do patrons search the online catalog when no one's looking? Transaction log analysis and implications for bibliographic instruction and system design. *RQ* 33 (Winter): 239–51.

Walter, Virginia A., Christine L. Borgman, and Sandra G. Hirsch. 1996. The science library catalog: Springboard for information literacy. *School Library Media Quarterly* 24 (Winter): 105–109.

Wilson, David L. 1994. Computer insecurity. *Chronicle of Higher Education* 40 (February): PA25–28.

Wright, Keith C. 1995. *Computer-related technologies in library operations.* Brookfield, VT: Gower.

Yurczyk, Judith. 1995. *MARC bibliographic format guide.* McHenry, IL: Follett Software Company.

Activity: Database Maintenance

Objective 1: To perform database maintenance on a media center or small library's automated system and to evaluate the quality of the database.

Description: 1. Select an automated system that is in full operation at a media center or a small library for which you would like to perform database maintenance. Detect errors in the following areas:

Author field. At random, select five MARC records that require corrections in the author fields. Check the indicator field for each main entry in tag 100 for correctness. Print out each record that needs correction and make the correction on each printout. Label each printout Author Field Correction.

Title field. At random, select five items with titles that start with initial articles (i.e., the, a, an, or another article). Check the indicator in tag 245 for correctness. Print out each record that requires correction and make the corrections on each printout. Label each printout Title Field Correction.

Subject headings. Select at least five subject headings that need correction. Print out each record and make the correction on each printout. Label each printout Subject Headings Correction.

Record filing. Scan a number of records by author, title, and subject in OPAC to verify their alphabetical filing. Identify the records that contain errors and print them. Use the cataloging module to examine the MARC record of each item that contains one or more errors. Print out each record and make the necessary corrections. Label each printout Record Filing in Subject Entries, Record Filing in Title Entries, or Record Filing in Author Entries, as applicable.

2. Evaluate the quality of the database.

7 ■ Networking

Networking involves connecting hardware devices for the purpose of exchanging information, software, printers, and other resources. Networking can increase the use of scarce resources, provide access to information outside a particular media center or library, and connect the media center or library to a worldwide audience via the Internet.

■ Types of Networks

A network may include minicomputers, microcomputers, mainframes or any combination of them. A network can be concentrated in one building or can spread out over several buildings close to one another in a local area network (LAN), or it can be spread over a larger geographic area in a metropolitan area network (MAN), or it can cross geographic boundaries in a wide area network (WAN). The major differences among these types of networks are geographic range and the speed of the connections. WANs, generally, have slower connections.

□ Local Area Networks (LANs)

A LAN may link offices, laboratories, and other facilities in one building or in buildings close to one another. Links among computers and peripherals can be achieved with coaxial cable, fiber optics, twisted-pair wire, or radio or infrared waves. The latter is the case with wireless LANs.

Sometimes, LANs are connected with other LANs to form an extended LAN. An example of such arrangement is the LAN in one department of an organization connected to the LAN in another department for the purpose of exchanging information that is needed by both departments.

There are two main types of LANs: peer-to-peer and file server.

Peer-to-Peer LANs

In a peer-to-peer network, computers are connected to one another to share files and printers without the use of a dedicated file server. Artisoft LANtastic, Appleshare, Novell's Netware Lite, Microsoft Windows for Workgroups, and Windows 95 are common operating systems for peer-to-peer networking.

Ease of installation and maintenance and low cost are the main advantages of peer-to-peer networks. The disadvantages of peer-to-peer networks reside in the limited number of computers that can be networked; ideally, this number is 10. As the number of computers increases, the network's performance decreases. Although this is true for all types of networks, it is more evident in peer-to-peer LANs than those that make use of a file server.

LANs Based on File Servers

This type of network connects many computers through a file server, or a dedicated computer. This arrangement is also called a client–server network. The client is the user's microcomputer, and the server is the file server, or the dedicated computer that stores the files and coordinates the exchange of information among the computers. Novell Netware, Microsoft Windows NT, and Banyan Vines are common operating systems for this type of networking.

The main advantage of a client–server network lies in its expandability; it can accommodate many computers without compromising performance. The disadvantages of a network system pertain to its complexity, cost of installation, frequent maintenance, and the need for dedicated machines to act as file servers.

☐ Metropolitan Area Network (MAN)

A MAN usually links computers in a city or region. Fiber optics, leased telephone lines, or radio or infrared transmission devices can be used to connect computers among buildings. For more information about MANs, see Manstel (1996) and Derfler and Freed (1993).

☐ Wide Area Network (WAN)

A WAN can be a nationwide or worldwide network. Satellites are used to establish communications among nodes, or earth stations. Earth stations may be linked to one another by microwave devices, cable, fiber optics, or telephone lines. The Internet is an example of a WAN that connects users around the world. Chapter 8 discusses the Internet in more detail.

■ Network Components

A network comprises three components: cabling, topology, and architecture. Cabling is like the highway system the data travels on. Topology is the physical layout of a network; it can be thought of as the design of various roads connected to a highway system. Architecture is best described as the rules of the road governing data that travels on the cabling.

☐ Network Cabling

There are three types of cabling systems: coaxial, twisted pair, and fiber optics. Cabling design and installation are extremely important for the proper operation of a network. The type of network cabling to use depends on the hardware platform, network topology, and the model chosen. Two cabling models are most common in media centers and libraries. The lab model consists of a cluster of computer workstations and a file server. The distributed model involves computer stations that are remote from the file server.

Cabling requires a well-planned design and proper installation. Poor implementation of a cabling system can result in data loss or slow performance.

Coaxial Cable

Coaxial cable has been used for high-frequency telegraph, telephone, and television signals. A type of coaxial cable is used to connect computer networks. Coaxial cable transports much information because of its large bandwidth. It is sturdy, resistant to electromagnetic interference (EMI), and transmits data at a speed up to 500 Mbps (megabytes per second). Coaxial cable is easy to install but bulky and relatively expensive.

Twisted Pair

Twisted-pair cable is used to support communication in telephone and networking systems. There are five categories of twisted-pair cable. Category 1 is used in a telephone system. Category 2 transmits data up to 1 MHz and, like Category 1 cable, it is not used in horizontal network cabling systems. Category 3 transports data up to 16 MHz and is typically used for voice and data transmission rates up to 10 Mbps. Category 3 represents the minimum transmission performance acceptable for horizontal cabling systems. Category 4 consists of cables and connectors specified up to 20 MHz and is intended for use with voice and data transmission for up to 20 Mbps. Category 5, which is

Table 7.1 Comparison of Cabling Options				
Criteria	STP	UTP	Coaxial	Fiber Optics
Cost	Moderate	Low	Moderate	High
Transmission	155Mbps	155Mbps	500Mbps	2GBps
Attenuation signal	100 meters	100 meters	1 kilometer	60 kilometers*
EMI	Good	Poor	Good	Excellent

*With repeaters.

the recommended level for networking, transmits data at 100 MHz at a rate over 150 Mbps (Automated Network Systems 1996).

There are two kinds of twisted pair cable: unshielded twisted pair (UTP) and shielded twisted pair (STP). UTP is a small, lightweight cable used in telephone connections and most LANs. It is inexpensive and relatively easy to install, but it is susceptible to data loss due to EMI, crosstalk among wires, and damage during installation. UTP has a limited bandwidth, signal attenuation (i.e., the length a signal can be carried) of 100 meters, and a data transmission speed of 155 Mbps.

STP is UTP with shielding. Unlike UTP, STP is bulky and heavy but rugged and reliable. Its shield provides excellent protection against EMI and crosstalk among wires. It has a limited bandwidth, however, and is also sensitive to damage during installation. STP has the same transmission speed and signal attenuation as UTP.

Fiber Optic Cable

Fiber optic cable is a small, lightweight cable with a large bandwidth. It provides excellent performance for high traffic, has a transmission speed of more than 2 Gbps (gigabits per second), and signal attenuation of more than 60 kilometers. Because it uses light to transmit signals, it is not subject to EMI. A fiber optic cable is less susceptible to damage during installation and has no grounding problems. Once prohibitively expense, the decrease in the cost of fiber optic cabling is making this option more affordable and more popular than UTP and STP for some LANs.

See table 7.1 for a comparison of various cabling options.

Cabling Installation

Because cables are vulnerable to interference from outside sources, special considerations must be made when cables are installed. Some of these considerations are

- Avoid running cables through areas in which there is heating and cooling equipment.

- Cover the cables with conduits or channels to minimize interference and to protect both users and cables.

- Terminate a cable at a junction box with the appropriate type of jack so that computer stations can be easily plugged into the network.

- Know where the existing electric, gas, bell, and alarm lines are located when drilling through a wall.

- Ensure that all cables meet all technical or standard specifications. Request the specifications from the company that is supplying your networking products.

- Employ certified technicians for cable installation (Automated Network Systems 1996).

□ Wireless LANs

A new trend in networking is wireless (cableless) LANs, which rely on radio or infrared waves instead of cable to link hardware devices. A standard for wireless LANs is being developed by the Institute of Electric and Electronic Engineers (IEEE). Selected companies for wireless and other LAN products are listed in table 7.2.

A wireless LAN allows flexibility in placing computers where they are needed and for moving them later. A wireless LAN is the preferred network for portable computers because it provides the performance of wired LANs but without the restrictions of cables. Usually, however, a wireless LAN complements an existing wired LAN in areas where running cable is expensive or impractical.

Wireless LAN products are becoming widespread; many companies have started to market them. AT&T WaveLAN, Solotek's Airlan, Digital Roam About, Aironet Arlan, Proxim's Range LAN2, RDC PortLAN, BreezeCOM's Breeze NET, and IBM Wireless LAN Entry are the leading products. The technology used in these products is the main differentiator among them. The most commonly used technologies are Direct-Sequence Spread-Spectrum (DSSS) and Frequency Hopping Spread-Spectrum (FHSS). A DSSS system sends data in bits simultaneously over a wide range of the spectrum, making it susceptible to radio interference. An FHSS system, however, sends data to one frequency then hops from one frequency to another, providing immunity to interference. The first four companies mentioned above use DSSS; the latter ones use FHSS (Boyle 1996).

Table 7.2 Selected Networking Companies

Name	Address	Web Address
Aironet Wireless Communications	367 Ghent Rd. Suite 300 Arkon, OH 44334 (800) 394-7353	http://www.aironet.com
ALLTEL Supply Inc.	6625 The Corners Parkway Norcross, GA 30092 (770) 448-5210	http://www.alltel.com
AT&T Network Systems	111 Madison Ave. Morristown, NJ 07960 (800) 344-0223	http://www.attgis.com
Automated Network Systems	365 Northridge Rd., Suite 480 Atlanta, GA 30350 (404) 804-4580	n/a
BreezeCOM	2195 Faraday Ave., Suite A Carlsbad, CA 92008 (619) 431-9880	http://www.breezecom.com
Digital Equipment Corporation	5 Littleton Rd. Westford, MA 01886 (800) 457-8211	http://www.networks.digital.com
Digital Ocean Inc.	11206 Thompson Ave. Lenexa, KS 66219 (800) 345-3474	http://www.digitalocean.com
IBM Corporation	700 Park Office Dr., Bldg. 662 Research Triangle Park, NC 27709 (800) 772-2227	http://www.raleigh.ibm.com
Microdyne Corporation	3601 Eisenhower Ave. Alexandria, VA 22304 (800) 255-3967	http://www.microdyne.com
Proxim Inc.	295 North Bernardo Ave. Mountain View, CA 94043 (800) 229-1630	http://www.proxim.com
RDC Networks	11 Beid Hadfus St. Foster City, CA 94404 (415) 577-8075	http://www.interop.com
Solectek Corporation	6370 Nancy Ridge Dr. #109 San Diego, CA 92121 (800) 437-1518	http://www.solectek.com
Waters Network Systems	2411 Seventh St., N.W. P.O. Box 6117 Rochester, MN 55903 (800) 441-5319	n/a

□ Network Topology

Network topology, or the physical layout of the network, can be designed as a bus, star, or ring layout.

Bus Topology

A bus topology consists of computers connected by a contiguous cable through which the information passes from one device to another. It is often used with small LANs and peer-to-peer networks. This topology may be used with or without a file server, as seen in figures 7.1 and 7.2. It does not require a hub or concentrator for connecting the computers. (A hub is a wiring device that contains multiple ports for connecting computers.) Troubleshooting the network is problematic, however, because any malfunction in the cable can disrupt communications across the whole network.

Star Topology

Star topology consists of computers connected to a file server that is linked to a hub or concentrator by cable or fiber optics (see figure 7.3). More than one hub may be used to accommodate a high number of connections (see figure 7.4). Similarly, more than one file server may be employed to serve high traffic. Because the computers in the network are connected to a hub rather than to each other, cabling problems are isolated and easy to detect. This makes troubleshooting relatively easy.

Ring Topology

In a ring topology, each computer is connected to two other computers to form a ring. Like the star, one or more file servers may be used. The main differences between this topology and the star is that data passes through the ring before it reaches its destination and one or more multiple access units (MAU) are employed instead of hubs. Figure 7.5 illustrates a token ring network wired in a star configuration, where the ring is located inside the MAU.

□ Network Architecture

The most common LAN architectures are: Ethernet, Token Ring, and Fiber Distributed Data Interface (FDDI). The key factors to consider in choosing a network design are the purpose of its use, existing and future applications, speed, reliability, security, ease of installation and maintenance, and cost.

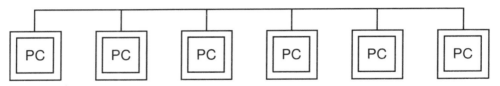

Figure 7.1 **Bus topology without a file server.**

PC = Personal computer

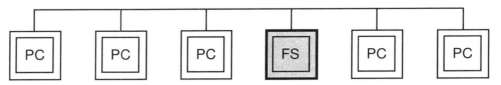

Figure 7.2 **Bus topology with a file server.**

PC = Personal computer
FS = File server

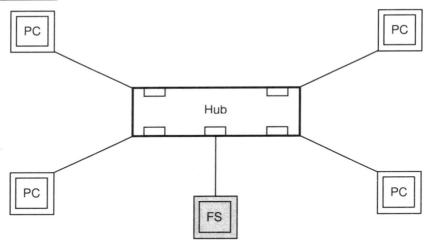

Figure 7.3 **Star topology.**

PC = Personal computer
FS = File server

Ethernet

Ethernet is one of the oldest and most widely used of the three types of network architecture. Ethernet is based on the Institute of Electrical and Electronics Engineers (IEEE) Carrier-Sense Multiple Access/Collision Detection (CSMA/CD) 802.3 standard. With collision detection, signals in every machine are transmitted during a break in the network traffic. When machines start transmitting at the same

Figure 7.4 **Star topology with multiple hubs.**

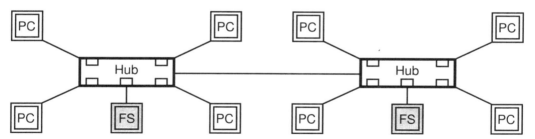

PC = Personal computer
FS = File server

Figure 7.5 **Ring topology.**

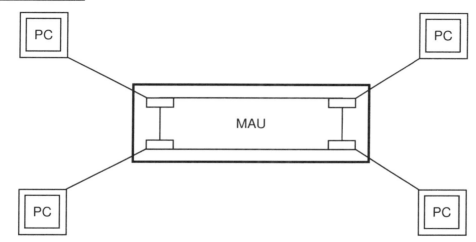

PC = Personal computer
MAU = Multiple Access Unit

time, they detect the collision, stop, and resubmit after a short period of time (Derfler and Freed 1993).

Each computer station in an Ethernet network requires a network interface card (NIC). This is also true for the other two architectures. Ethernet operates over fiber optics, STP and UTP, and coaxial cable; it features three baseband schemes: 10Base2 (10 Mbps) up to 185 meters in distance per segment (ideally, 5 segments exist on a network); 10Base5 (10 Mbps and up to 500 meters); and 10BaseT (10 Mbps using STP, UTP, or fiber optics with 100 meters in distance from a hub to a workstation). Ethernet is reliable, inexpensive, and can be implemented with various topologies. When more than two computer stations are communicating, however, data may need to be sent at least twice due to collision with other traffic, making the transmission at less than 10 Mbps (Waters Network Systems 1996).

Token Ring

Token Ring is an IBM LAN architecture that uses a Token-passing technology, which allows all communications to pass through the ring to determine whether each connected hardware device has a message to transmit. Each message is then sent to the next connected device until it reaches its destination.

A Token Ring LAN is based on IEEE standard 802.5. It operates over STP, UTP, or fiber optics at a speed of 4 or 16 Mbps. It is considered the most cost-efficient architecture because of its consistent performance, effective management of data transmission over a network, reliability, accommodation of high workloads, and absence of collision.

Token is expensive in terms of both materials (i.e., cable, hub, and network cards) and maintenance (i.e., labor). It is more sophisticated to troubleshoot than Ethernet, but is more fault-tolerant and reliable.

Fiber Distributed Data Interface (FDDI)

FDDI LAN is the most expensive networking architecture of the three. It uses a Token-passing technology, runs at 100 Mbps, and can extend up to 60 miles in distance. FDDI's excellent performance makes it ideal for a network's backbone. Its high cost is its main drawback.

■ Summary

A LAN can be located in one place (e.g., a media center), or it can be part of a building-level or campus-level LAN (e.g., a LAN connected to another LAN via a bridge). A LAN can also be part of a MAN (e.g., a LAN connected to a MAN via a modem or fiber optics), or part of a WAN (e.g., a LAN connected to the Internet via a modem, ISDN, T-1).

The selection of a LAN cabling system (e.g., STP, UTP, coaxial, fiber optics), a topology (e.g., bus, star, ring), and an architecture (e.g., Ethernet, Token Ring, FDDI) should be based on the following factors: the media center's or library's existing and future applications, the data transmission speed desired, reliability, security, ease of installation and maintenance, and affordability. Each cabling system, topology, and architecture has advantages and disadvantages, which should be carefully examined in relation not only to the media center's or library's needs and requirements, but also the needs and requirements of the host institution.

Qualified personnel should be available on site to diagnose and troubleshoot the network problems so that user access is not hampered. To maintain the network's long-term reliability and to reduce the money and time spent on its maintenance, consider hiring certified personnel to design and install the cabling system, even though it is expensive.

■ References

Automated Network Systems. 1996. *Communication cabling and installation.* Atlanta, GA: Automated Network Systems.

Boyle, Padraic R. 1996. Wireless LANs: Free to roam. *PC Magazine* (February 20). http://www.pcmag.com/issues/. (Accessed June 6, 1996.)

———. 1996. Solectek Corp.: Airlan. *PC Magazine* (February 20). Available: http://www.pcmag.com/issues/1504/pcm00096.html. (Accessed June 6, 1996.)

Derfler, Frank J., Jr., and Les Freed. 1993. *How networks work.* Emerville, CA: Ziff-Davis Press.

Manstel, Vern L. 1996. Building a school district's Wide Area Network. *T.H.E. Journal* 23 (April): 69–75.

Morgan, Rick. 1996. Network technology. Valdosta, GA: Educational Technology Training Center, Valdosta State University. Unpublished.

O'Leary, Timothy J., and Linda I. O'Leary. 1995. *Computing essentials.* New York: McGraw-Hill.

PC Magazine The entire February 20, 1996, issue is devoted to wireless LANs.

Pompili, Tony. 1996. Digital Equipment Corp.: RoamAbout. *PC Magazine* (February 20). http://www.pcmag.com/issues/. (Accessed June 6, 1996.)

Quain, John R. 1996. AT&T network systems: WaveLAN. *PC Magazine* (February 20). http://www.pcmag.com/issues/. (Accessed June 6, 1996.)

———. 1996. IBM Corp.: IBM wireless LAN entry. *PC Magazine* (February 20). http://www.pcmag.com/issues/. (Accessed June 6, 1996.)

Waters Network Systems. 1996. *Network solutions for education.* Rochester, MN: Waters Network Systems.

Witt, Jeffrey G. 1996. What the numbers mean. *PC Magazine* (February 20). http://www.pcmag.com/pclabs/network/n1504wa.html. (Accessed June 6, 1996.)

Activity: Networking

Objective 1:   To explore a LAN's hardware and software requirements.

Description: 1.   Select a media center or a small library that has a LAN in place. Make an appointment with the person who is knowledgeable about the LAN (e.g., the media specialist, the technology specialist, the technology coordinator, or other personnel). Ask questions to learn the following about the LAN:

> topology (e.g., star, bus, ring);
>
> cabling system (e.g., coaxial, twisted pair, fiber optics);
>
> architecture (e.g., Ethernet, Token Ring, FDDI);
>
> the network's operating system software (e.g., Netware, AppleShare, Windows NT);
>
> the workstation operating system (e.g., DOS, Windows, MAC);
>
> the kind of workstations (e.g., PC-compatible, Macintosh);
>
> the brand name of the workstations, their RAM, hard drive capacity, and type of microprocessors;
>
> the kind of file servers used (e.g., PC-compatible, Macintosh);
>
> the brand name of the file server, its RAM size, hard drive capacity, and type of microprocessors; and
>
> the type (e.g., laser, dot matrix, inkjet, color) and brand name of printers;

2. Write a report describing the LAN, based on your research.

Objective 2: To evaluate the performance and capacity of a LAN with respect to its existing and future applications.

Description: 1. Evaluate the capacity of the LAN selected for Objective One with regard to both existing applications and future applications (e.g., to support video, voice, and data; to add CD-ROM databases, to support Internet access).

2. Draw a map of the LAN's layout and components, including the placement of workstations; the file server; printer(s); the CD-ROM tower; and other components and hardware.

3. Write a report of your evaluation; include the map of the LAN.

8 OPACs on the Internet

■ Microcomputer-based automated systems have recently entered a new phase of technological development by becoming accessible on the World Wide Web (Web or WWW) and by complying with the Z39.50 standard.

For the last few years, access to online catalogs on the Internet, especially those for K-12 libraries, has been limited to Hytelnet. Recently, K-12 OPACs have become available on the World Wide Web, a hypertext-based Internet server containing links to related resources on the Internet. Unlike other servers (i.e., Gopher, Archie, and WAIS), the Web has the ability to integrate text, images, and sound. To take full advantage of its hypermedia capability, one must have a browser, such as Netscape, Microsoft Internet Explorer, or Mosaic.

■ The Internet

Libraries that wish to make their online catalogs available in cyberspace must have Internet access, and their automation software must include the Transmission Control Protocol/Internet Protocol (TCP/IP).

The Internet is a network of networks that connects millions of computer systems and people. The Internet offers the benefits of exchanging messages using electronic mail (e-mail), searching a variety of databases, downloading files, exchanging information using mailing lists and bulletin boards, and logging into remote systems. It also supports videoconferencing and vocal communications (or chats).

The TCP/IP protocol facilitates communications among various computer networks, regardless of the operating systems, languages, and hardware employed. It breaks down data sent over the Internet into small packets and sends it to its address or destination through networks connected to the Internet (Meghabghab 1996). In simple terms, this protocol can be thought of in two portions: TCP can be thought of as a post office and IP as a home address.

141

□ Connecting to the Internet

Connecting to the Internet can be done in a number of ways. Most media centers and libraries qualify for access through a statewide network or Freenet. Commercial online service providers, such as CompuServe and America Online, also offer access, as do telephone (and some cable television) companies and Internet service providers (ISPs) who specialize in providing access to the Internet. It is beyond the scope of this book to discuss connecting to the Internet, Internet servers, and services; many Internet primers include this information. The reader is referred to sources in the list of references by MacDonald (1997), Ryder and Hughes (1997), and Grauer (1996). A directory of Internet companies (Newsome 1997) is a good source for finding companies that provide access to the Internet.

■ Access to OPACs in Cyberspace

OPACs in cyberspace can be accessed via Hytelnet and on the World Wide Web. Hytelnet is a software program written by Peter Scott, manager of small systems at the University of Saskatchewan Libraries in Saskatoon, Canada. Hytelnet is a database of online catalogs for all types of libraries that are accessible via telnet. It also includes links to a variety of Internet resources and online databases in the public domain.

Telnet is a protocol that handles the communication between a local computer and any remote host computer running a telnet server (Scott 1997). Hytelnet and telnet must be installed on the user's computer system and the host system the user's computer is networked to. If Hytelnet is available for access on your computer, you can find OPACs by performing the following steps:

1. Connect to your host computer system.

2. Type *hytelnet* at the host system's prompt and press the Enter or Return key. This command will return a menu similar to the following. (All example menus in the section are from the Valdosta State University system.)

Key-stroke commands	\<HELP\>
VSU Odum Library	\<DRAGON\>
Peachnet Gopher	\<PGOPHER\>
VSU Electronic Services	\<SERVICES\>
University of Georgia Library	\<UGALIB\>
University System Union Library Catalog	\<UNION\>
Ga. Southern University Information Services	\<GASOU\>
Other Library Catalogs	\<SITES1\>
Other Resources	\<SITES2\>

3. From the menu choose Other Library Catalogs <SITES 1>.
    A menu similar to the following menu will appear on your
    screen:

<SITES1A>	The Americas
<SITES1B>	Europe/Scandinavia
<SITES1C>	Asia/Pacific/South Africa

4. Select <SITES1A> The Americas. A menu similar to the
    following menu will appear on your screen:

<BR000>	Brazil
<CA000>	Canada
<CL000>	Chile
<MX000>	Mexico
<US000>	United States
<VE000>	Venezuela

5. Select <US000> United States. A listing of all types of
    libraries will appear on your screen:

Consortia	<US000CON>
Other Libraries	<US0000TH>
Law Libraries	<US000LAW>
Medical Libraries	<US000MED>
Public Libraries	<US000PUB>
Community College Libraries	<US000COM>
K–12 Libraries	<US000K12>

6. Select the type of library you would like to search. You will
    be asked to confirm the telnet command and identify your
    computer terminal type. Follow the directions for logging in.

Some K-12 OPACs are Archbishop Carroll High School (Pennsylvania), Chaoate Rosemary Hall High School (Connecticut), Fayetteville School District (Arkansas), Hotchkiss School (Connecticut), Kaplan Elementary School (Louisiana), Kent School (Connecticut), Mary Institute/Country Day (Missouri), Onondaga-Cortland-Madison BOCES (New York), SUNLINK/Florida K-12 Library Union Database, St. Paul's School (New Hampshire), and Unified School District 465 (Kansas).

Libraries that wish to make their online catalogs telnet-accessible, should contact Peter Scott by e-mail (pscott@library.berkeley.edu), by phone (306-966-5920), or by fax (306-966-6040). You may also want to access his home page at (http://www.usask.ca/~scottp).

Recently, Hytelnet became available for access on the World Wide Web at (http://library.usask.ca/hytelnet). This Web page is an interface to the same Hytelnet, but in a Windows environment, meaning that selecting an OPAC to search will generate a telnet command to the OPAC through the Web.

■ The World Wide Web

Many libraries' OPACs are on the Web and searchable in a Windows environment. WebCATS (http://librry.usask.ca/hywebcat) is a list of K-12 OPACs created by Peter Scott and Doug Macdonald at the University of Saskatchewan Libraries. Libweb (http://sunsite.Berkeley.edu/Libweb) is a list of more than 1,428 home pages from libraries in 62 countries (Dowling 1997), including special and school libraries. A library that wishes to add its OPAC URL to Libweb should contact Thomas Dowling by e-mail (tdowling@ohiolink.edu) or submit the URL from the appropriate place on the Libweb home page.

K-12 OPACs can also be found by searching the Web 66 site (http://web66.coled.umn.edu/schools.html), a registry of national and international schools on the Web, and School Libraries on the Web Directory (http://www.voicenet.com/~bertland/libs.html), which is a list of home pages of K-12 schools worldwide. You can submit your OPAC's URL to either listing from the appropriate place on their home pages.

URL addresses of individual OPACs can be found by performing a keyword, phrase, or Boolean search in any Web engine (e.g., Yahoo, Lycos, Magellan, WebCrawler). If a specific OPAC is part of a consortium of OPACs, it is wise to search under the name of the consortium. Georgia Library Learning Online (GALILEO) is an example of a consortium that provides access to all Georgia OPACs in addition to a variety of reference databases and information related to Georgia. The GALILEO address is http://galileo.gsu.edu. Additional OPACs can be located through the Library of Congress (LC) Web site at http://lcweb.loc.gov.

■ Searching OPACs with the Z39.50 Standard

Automated systems vary with regard to hardware, operating systems and platforms, and applications software used. Because of these variations, the search commands, features, and screen displays for various OPACs differ from one to another. The Z39.50 standard allows systems to execute, retrieve, and display information in one common format, regardless of the hardware, software, platform, database structure, content, or format employed in a particular system. The Z39.50 standard also applies to reference databases. Additional information about this standard can be found at http://www.markkelly.com/z3950.

The Library of Congress Z39.50 Gateway (http://lcweb.loc.gov/z3950/gateway.html) contains links to many Z39.50 standard OPACs. The most notable ones are those sponsored by Data Research Associates (DRA), INNOPAC, NOTIS, SIRSI, the Colorado Alliance of Research Libraries (CARL), and GEAC. The application of the Z39.50 standard in microcomputer-based automated systems is provided in Bibliofile ITS for Windows from The Library Corporation. Software vendors in the process of implementing this standard are Winnebago Software Company and SIRS. Winnebago Spectrum is expected to be released in 1997; SIRS Mandarin was scheduled for release in summer 1997. The application of Z39.50 standard to microcomputer-based automated systems is expected to increase as versions of the automation software become available in Windows and Windows NT, and as they become compatible with TCP/IP protocol for access over the Internet.

The leading Z39.50 standard reference databases are those provided by OCLC and DRA. A minimum of 13 subdatabases are available from OCLC through its FirstSearch database. Examples are: Applied Science and Technology Index, Business Periodicals Index, Education Index, and Reader's Guide Abstracts. More than six Z39.50 standard subdatabases are available from DRA through its DRANET database. The Library of Congress MARC database, Business Index, General Periodicals Index, and Magazine Index Plus are examples of databases available from DRA.

The implementation of the Z39.50 standard, which standardizes the appearance and command functions of OPACs over the Internet, has made it possible for users to search various OPACs using one command interface and command language, thus making OPACs from around the world easier to search.

■ Making Your OPAC Available on the Web

Libraries wishing to make their OPAC available for access on the Web will need

> a Windows-based automation software with TCP/IP protocol;
>
> MS-Windows software;
>
> a web browser, such as Netscape, Microsoft Internet Explorer, or Mosaic;
>
> Internet access;
>
> a Web (URL) address; and
>
> a Web link software compatible with the automation software. Such software is available from automation software companies.

A web-ready OPAC should be indexed in services like Libweb or WebCATS so that it will be included in lists of OPACs. This will help users find the OPAC. You can submit your OPAC's URL to Libweb through the Libweb home page (http://sunsite.Berkeley.edu/Libweb); submission to WebCATS is available online from the WebCATS home page or by contacting Peter Scott by e-mail at scott@moondog. usask.ca.

□ Web Link Software

The leading microcomputer-based automated systems with Web link software compatible with their automated systems are: Nichols Advanced Technologies (Athena Weblink); The Library Corporation (Bibliofile Net PAC); Brodart Automation (Le PAC Net); and Auto-Graphics (Impact/ONLINE Web PAC). As Windows versions of automation software increase, it is expected that automation software companies will make their software Web-ready in the near future.

■ Benefits of OPACs in Cyberspace

OPACs in cyberspace offer a wide array of benefits as they open new avenues for global information access and increased accessibility to library collections. Indeed, any user with Internet access can search OPACs from any remote location. Users are no longer confined to the local boundaries of media centers or libraries; they can access OPACs from homes, offices, or elsewhere, and they access OPACs around the clock. They can identify the materials they need, determine whether the materials are available in their local libraries, and issue interlibrary loan (ILL) requests for borrowing materials not available locally. Appropriate ILL forms can be generated and completed online through a library's home page and mailed directly to the lending library.

Bibliofile Net PAC is an example of software that provides such an OPAC. A hyperlink feature built into Net PAC's MARC enables users to click on a hyper keyword or term and initiate new searches for that keyword or term without returning to the keyword search menu. Brodart Automation Company, the sponsor of Le Pac Net, is also developing the interlibrary loan and hypertext searching features. A demo of Net PAC is available at http://www.tlcdelivers.com; Le Pac Net can be accessed at http://www.brodart.com.

OPACs in cyberspace serve as gateways to the vast amount of information available on the Internet. Access to libraries' union catalogs (a collection of districtwide or statewide online catalogs) and to other OPACs encourages resource sharing among libraries, thus reducing the cost of collection development. Online OPACs also provide media specialists and information professionals with new means for evaluating their library collections; they can compare their collections to those of other libraries. Additional benefits relate to the access of millions of bibliographic MARC records available on the Internet; these records can be used for cataloging and verifying ILL requests. The Library of Congress provides full access to its catalog (LOCIS) MARC database, which contains more than 27 million records. Full access to these records is available via telnet at (locis.loc.gov). Partial access (3.8 million records) and the name authority file (3.6 million records) are available on the Web (http://lcweb.loc.gov). Additional sites for access to MARC records is provided through the Librarians Information Online Network Online (LION) Catalogs and Bibliographic Services at (http://www.libertynet.org/online-catalogs.html). The LION home page is an excellent resource for locating information about many subjects for school libraries.

In the chaotic world of the Internet, OPACs offer a well-structured and organized subworld where information is classified, indexed, and retrieved according to established standards. This is important, because even experienced searchers find it difficult to locate specific information on the Internet, especially the World Wide Web. As media centers and other libraries become hubs of information, they will need to shift their focus from local information access to global information access. OPACs in cyberspace are ideal information tools that not only provide users with access to earthly information, but also empower them with online searching skills that are needed to unravel this world of information.

■ Summary

The presence of OPACs in cyberspace serves as a gateway to global information and encourages resource sharing among libraries. The availability of many reference and other resources on the Internet, as well as resource sharing, however, may prompt administrators to cut media centers' budget for collection development. Therefore, media specialists should clarify to their administrators the reciprocal borrowing and lending involved in resource sharing and the volatility of reference and other resources on the Internet. The use of Internet resources should supplement collection development rather than substitute for it.

Wide access to U.S. MARC records, as well as other resources on the Internet, raises the issue of copyright, which needs to be dealt with by all media specialists and librarians.

Windows-based K-12 OPACs on the Web possess advanced features over their DOS-based counterparts. The capability of these OPACs to perform hyperword searching, issue interlibrary loan forms, provide document delivery online, and comply with the Z39.50 standard will make microcomputer-based automated systems competitive with minicomputer-based and mainframe-based systems. Although these advanced features are still limited to a few microcomputer-based automation software packages, the number of software packages with these features is expected to increase in the near future.

■ References

Ackerman, Ernest. 1995. *Learning to use the Internet*. Wilsonville, OR: Franklin, Beedle & Associates.

Dowling, Thomas. 1997. Libweb's home page. Copyright 1996. http://sunsite.Berkeley.edu/Libweb. (Accessed February 19, 1997).

Eager, Bill. 1994. *Using the world wide web*. Indianapolis, IN: Que.

Epler, Doris, ed. 1995. *K-12 networking: Breaking the walls of the learning environment*. Medford, NJ.: Information Today.

Grauer, Marx. 1996. *Exploring the Internet*. Englewood Cliffs, NJ: Prentice Hall.

Librarians Information Online Network (LION) home page. No copyright. http://www.libertynet.org/~lion/lion.html. (Accessed February 24, 1997.)

MacDonald, Randall M. 1997. *The Internet and the school library media specialist: Transforming traditional services*. Westport, CT: Greenwood Publishing.

Meghabghab, George V. 1996. *Introduction to UNIX*. Indianapolis, IN: Que.

Newsome, Colin, ed. 1997. *Major Internet companies 1997*. New York: American Educational Systems.

Ryder, Randall J., and Tom Hughes. 1997. *Internet for educators*. Upper Saddle River, N.J.: Merrill.

Scott, Peter. 1997. Hytelnet home page. No copyright. http://www.usask.ca/~scottp. (Accessed February 19, 1997.)

Activity: Access to Z39.50 OPACs

Objective 1: To gain experience in searching Z39.50 OPACs in cyberspace.

Description: 1. Connect to the Library of Congress Z39.50 Gateway at http://lcweb.loc.gov/z3950/gateway.html.

2. Select one DRA and one SIRSI OPAC or database to search.

3. Perform one search in each OPAC by:

    author,

    title,

    subject,

    keyword (use Boolean logic), and

    phrase.

4. Print the results of each search in each OPAC.

5. Compare the search commands and features applied in each OPAC.

Objective 2: To compare a Z39.50 OPAC to an OPAC that is not in compliance with this standard.

Description: 1. Select one OPAC that is not in compliance with the Z39.50 standard. You may use Hytelnet or WWW to locate the OPAC.

2. Conduct a search for each of the following:

    author,

    title,

    subject,

    keyword (use Boolean logic), and

    phrase.

3. Compare the search commands and features of this OPAC to the Z39.50 OPAC you previously searched.

4. Elaborate on the advantages and disadvantages of Z39.50 OPACs based on your experience.

5. Write a report describing your experience and comparing the two types of OPACs.

⁹ Future OPACs

The 1990s have been marked by a digital revolution, which has dramatically reshaped the way information is accessed and utilized. As the very nature of information changes, so does the role of all libraries, from ownership of information to access to information, and from acquiring and housing technologies to pathfinders of information. This chapter describes the current status and issues related to OPACs and provides recommendations for improvement of future OPACs.

■ Present Status of OPACs

Today's OPACs have progressed from a replica of a card catalog to an information gateway. The abilities of OPACs far exceed searching a collection by author, title, and subject; today's OPACs can also be searched using keywords, Boolean logic, and natural language. In addition, the development of PC-based client/server architecture has made possible the implementation of Z39.50 standard OPACs on the Internet. Most recently, WorldPAC, a new software for wrapping MARC records with HyperText Markup Language (HTML), was released by Electronic On-line Systems International to facilitate OPAC access on the World Wide Web (Cheatham 1996).

One cannot underestimate the progress OPACs have made in the last decade and a half. The problems OPACs are still afflicted with, however, should not be overlooked. Since 1983, when the first use study of online catalogs was conducted by the Council on Library Resources (CLR), online catalogs have suffered from subject access problems. The CLR study showed that 43 percent of users experienced difficulties with subject searching (Matthews, Lawrence, and Ferguson 1983). Studies that followed echoed the CLR findings and further revealed that keyword searching, use of Boolean logic, query formulation, information overload, and management of the information retrieved for the purpose of broadening or narrowing search results were major problems (Bates 1986;

151

Blazek and Bilal 1988; Borgman 1986; Markey 1986; Edmonds, Moore, and Balcom 1990; Hunter 1991; Chen 1991; Larson 1992; Solomon 1993).

In an article entitled "Knowledge Navigation and Librarians in the Word Fray," Hovde (1996) commented about the problems with searching online catalogs. In online searches, she maintains, "researchers have noted that as many as one-third of the subject queries users enter into online catalogs fail to produce retrieval" (p. 9). Moreover, when keyword searching was successful, users were confronted with information overload. These studies suggest that subject access, keyword searching, and query formulation are the most pressing issues to be solved in OPACs.

■ Future OPACs

Future OPACs are expected to act as intelligent servers to global information access. As such, OPACs should store, retrieve, and model the knowledge of expert information providers (i.e., media specialists, reference librarians, and information specialists). Improving access in future OPACs requires the efforts of both system designers and information providers.

□ Role of System Designers

Research concerning OPAC developments and enhancements is well documented by O'Brien (1994). Her thorough literature review revealed no evidence of studies of the role of information providers as an essential component in solving access problems with OPACs. Studies of information-seeking behavior reveal that users' knowledge of their information needs during the initial stages of the search process are imprecise and uncertain. When a user approaches an information professional for assistance, an information provider attempts to identify a user's true information need through query negotiation. After the need is identified, the information provider recommends appropriate answer-providing tools and helps the user select proper concepts to include in a query statement. When users access OPACs without the help of an information provider, they may query the system poorly.

In 1968, Taylor described the first level of a user's need as the unexpressed need. In 1981, Belkin characterized a patron's early search process as anomalous and lacking sufficient knowledge to specify the precise need. In 1991, Kuhlthau described users' perspectives of the initial stages of the information search process as vague, uncertain, and accompanied by frustration and confusion. These results suggest that system vendors and designers should become aware of the cognitive processes of information seekers to use as a framework for providing innovative access techniques. These techniques should include modeling and implementing the reference query negotiation process by using expert systems or neural networks. Researchers who investigate new designs and techniques for improving access problems, especially subject searching, should consider these techniques as well.

In *Knowledge-Based Systems for General Reference Work,* Richardson (1995) describes more than 10 expert system shells for knowledge representation and for customizing knowledge-based information systems. In their study of the application of the reference process in OPACs, Meghabghab and Meghabghab (1994) proposed a design model for intelligent query negotiation using neural networks. Neural networks are related to artificial intelligence; their processing capability and power of learning adaptiveness allows them to perform human-like intelligence tasks. The researchers also recommended that a neural network shell be trained to execute analogical reasoning similar to that performed by expert information providers.

Additional enhancements for future OPACs should embrace the following:

- Natural language searching and translation of natural language queries into an automated system's controlled vocabulary.

- Online assistance of concept selection relevant to a user's query.

- Relevance ranking of retrieved results.

- Increase in the application of Windows-based software as well as PC-based client/server architecture with Z39.50 capability.

- Meaningful icons in Windows-based OPACs and significant connections between images and words.

- Innovative user interfaces with user profiles. Modeling users will allow an OPAC to identify a user's level of knowledge and interest. This interface is especially needed in children's catalogs.

- User feedback to alert the user about errors in search statements and to provide remediation, rather than returning zero hits.

- Online assistance with query formulation and search strategies related to a user's query.

- Comprehensive tutorials with illustrated examples of various types of searches. Tutorials for both novice and advanced users should be included. The incorporation of multimedia in tutorials designed for children should also be considered.

- The ability to forgive spacing and misspelling, to ignore stop words, and to automatically strip stop words from search statements.

- A transaction log of search statements to include not only the number of searches performed, but also the type of search statements entered into the system so that problem areas are addressed in user training.

- Authority control.

- Hyperword searching.

Most of these enhancements are needed in microcomputer-based automated systems.

☐ Role of Information Providers

Information providers are constantly in direct contact with their users. They serve as trainers, consultants, and information managers. Users go to information providers for assistance to locate information. Therefore, information providers should assume a leadership role in studying their users' information-seeking behavior to unravel strengths and weaknesses. This endeavor will not only provide guidance for designing and developing adequate end-user training programs, but will also identify key problems to communicate to system vendors and designers.

Information providers must adopt sound end-user training programs for OPAC use. Such programs may include search strategy formulation, concept selection, controlled vocabulary versus free-text searching, use of Boolean operators, record structure, and evaluation and management of document retrieval. Equipping users with these skills will allow them to expand their search skills beyond a local OPAC to online information systems, such as the World Wide Web.

As libraries move toward the virtual libraries concept, they will deliver a wide array of digital resources. "It would be an imperative . . . [that the creators of these libraries] think in terms of a single point of access, 'one stop shopping'. . . to the digital store" (Kochtanek 1995, p. 81).

Information providers must shift from the traditional mode of thinking, organizing, and retrieving information to innovative approaches in packaging and delivering information services. As Lynch (1994) contends, librarians should be "more flexible in abandoning traditional bibliographic apparatus." End users' needs will also be transformed in the digital age. O'Brien (1994) maintains that "end users [will] demand a catalog that resembles less the traditional manual model, not just in how it displays information but more critically in how it searches" (p. 236).

Indeed, only successful information providers will survive. As Crawford and Gorman (1995) argue, "There will only be successful libraries in the future—because, if libraries are not successful, they will cease to exist" (p. 178).

■ References

American National Standard Institute and National Information Standards Organization. 1995. *American National Standard Information Retrieval Application Service Definition and Protocol Specifications for Open Systems Interconnection.* (ANSI/NISO Z39.50.) Bethesda, MD: National Information Standards Office.

Bates, M. 1986. Subject access in online catalogs: A design model. *Journal of the American Society for Information Science* 37 (6): 357–76.

Belkin, N. J. 1981. ASK for information retrieval: Part I. Background and theory. *Journal of Documentation* 38: 61–71.

Blazek, R., and Dania Bilal. 1988. Problems with OPAC: A case study of an academic library. *RQ* 28 (2): 169–78.

Borgman, Christine L. 1986. Why are online catalogs hard to use? Lessons learned from information retrieval studies. *Journal of the American Society for Information Science* 37 (6): 384–400.

Cheatham, Scot A. 1996. Open your OPAC to WWW access with WorldPAC. *Input / Output: The Newsletter of EOS International* 12 (1): 1–4.

Chen, Shu-Hsien. 1991. A study of online catalog searching behavior of high school students. Ed.D. diss., University of Georgia.

Crawford, Walt. 1993. The future online catalog: A single view of multiple databases. *Information Technology and Libraries* 12 (2): 253–54.

Crawford, Walt, and Michael Gorman. 1995. *Future libraries: Dreams, madness, and reality.* Chicago: American Library Association.

Drabenstott, Karen Markey. 1996. Enhancing a new design for subject access to online catalogs. *Library High Tech* 14 (1): 87–109.

Edmonds, Leslie, Paula Moore, and Kathleen M. Balcom. 1990. The effectiveness of an online catalog. *School Library Journal* 36 (October): 28–32.

Hovde, Karen. 1996. Knowledge navigation and librarians in the word fray. *Bulletin of the American Society for Information Science* 22 (6): 8–10.

Hunter, Rhonda N. 1991. Successes and failures of patrons searching the online catalog at a large academic library: A transaction log analysis. *RQ* 30 (3): 395–402.

Kochtanek, Thomas R. 1995. Open systems considerations for integrated online library systems. *Proceedings of the Tenth Integrated Online Library Systems Meeting,* New York, May, pp. 77–84.

Kuhlthau, Carol C. 1991. Inside the search process: Information seeking from the user's perspective. *Journal of the American Society for Information Science* 42 (5): 361–71.

Larson, R. R. 1992. Evaluation of advanced retrieval techniques in an experimental online catalog. *Journal of the American Society for Information Science* 43 (1): 34–53.

Lynch, Clifford. 1994. Keynote speech. Ninth Integrated Online Library Systems Meeting, New York, May 12.

Markey, Karen. 1986. Users and the online catalog: Subject access problems. In *The impact of online catalogs*. Edited by J. R. Matthews. New York: Neal-Schuman, pp. 35–70.

Matthews, Joseph R., Gary S. Lawrence, and Douglas K. Ferguson, eds. 1983. *Using online catalogs: A nationwide survey.* New York: Neal-Schuman.

Meghabghab, George V., and Dania B. Meghabghab. 1994. INN: An intelligent negotiating neural network for information systems: A design model. *Information Processing and Management* 30 (5): 663–85.

O'Brien, Ann. 1994. Online catalogs: Enhancements and developments. *Annual Review of Information Science and Technology* 29: 219–42.

Richardson, John V., Jr. 1995. *Knowledge-based systems for general reference work.* Chicago: American Library Association.

Solomon, Paul. 1993. Children's information retrieval behavior: A case analysis of an OPAC. *Journal of the American Society for Information Science* 44 (5): 245–64.

Taylor, Robert S. 1968. Question-negotiation and information seeking in libraries. *College and Research Libraries* 29: 178–94.

Glossary

AACR2R: *Anglo-American Cataloguing Rules, Second Revised Edition* (1988). A bibliographic standard that is based on a set of rules used to describe various types of library materials.

Alliance Plus: A CD-ROM database of MARC records developed by Follett Software Company. It is mainly used for retrospective conversion.

arithmetic-logic unit: A part of the central processing unit that carries out mathematical computations and logic operations.

authority control: The process of grouping variant forms of a heading under one single heading for the purpose of maintaining consistency. Authority control applies to personal author names, corporate bodies, subject headings, and series.

barcode: A set of numbers represented by a pattern of bars that can be recognized by automation software. Barcodes are assigned to an item or a patron. A barcode can be entered electronically using a hardware device (i.e., a barcode scanner) or manually by typing the numbers into an automated system.

barcode scanner: Hardware used to scan, read, and/or enter a barcode number into an automated system.

Bibliofile: A CD-ROM database of MARC records developed by the Library Corporation. It is mainly used for retrospective conversion.

Boolean logic: Logic based on Boolean algebra. It was developed by the logician George Boole. The main functions used in information retrieval are the operators *and* to narrow search results, *or* to expand search results, and *not* to narrow search results by eliminating unwanted terms. *See also* nesting.

Boolean operators: *See* Boolean logic, nesting.

bus: A device that connects internal hardware (e.g., CPU, printer control unit) or external hardware devices (e.g., stations in a network).

byte: Eight bits that represent a character, such as a letter, symbol, or number.

cache: A section of the random access memory (RAM) that functions to provide faster information retrieval.

CD-ROM: *See* compact disc read-only memory.

central processing unit (CPU): A unit in the computer that stores and processes the data. It consists of two main units: the control unit and the arithmetic-logic unit.

client-server: A client is any computer connected to a network. A server is a computer station that stores the software that a client accesses.

compact disc read-only memory (CD-ROM): A read-only optical disc that stores a pre-recorded piece of software. A CD-ROM program cannot be altered or erased.

control unit: A part of the central processing unit that receives program instructions and instructs the rest of the computer how to execute these instructions.

CPU: *See* central processing unit.

EISA: *See* Extended Industry Standard Architecture.

Eudora: A PC-based software program for using electronic mail (e-mail) over the Internet.

Extended Industry Standard Architecture (EISA): A bus standard for IBM-compatible computers. It allows more than one central processing unit (CPU) to share the bus.

file transfer protocol (FTP): A standard for exchanging and downloading files over the Internet.

FTP: *See* file transfer protocol.

GALILEO: *See* Georgia Library Learning Online.

Georgia Library Learning Online (GALILEO): A database for universal access to materials and information services to students and faculty in the University of Georgia system.

Georgia Online Database (GOLD): A statewide bibliographic utility for resource sharing among system libraries in the state of Georgia.

gigabyte: One billion bytes.

GOLD: *See* Georgia Online Database.

graphical user interface (GUI): Software that allows users to interface with software through the use of icons, graphics, and textual information. This contrasts with character- or text-based interfaces (e.g., DOS, Lynx).

GUI: *See* graphical user interface.

home page: The first screen one sees when connecting to a site on the World Wide Web.

HTML: *See* Hypertext Markup Language.

http: *See* Hypertext Transfer Protocol.

Hypertext Markup Language (HTML): Code used to write hypertext documents (often for the World Wide Web).

Hypertext Transfer Protocol (http): A standard used for accessing sites, particularly World Wide Web sites, on the Internet. The abbreviation http appears at the beginning of a site address.

Hytelnet: A tool for accessing resources via Telnet on the Internet.

Integrated Service Digital Network (ISDN): A standard for transmitting information (data, voice, and video) over a digital communications line. This method of transmitting data is much faster than transmitting data over a traditional telephone line.

integrated software: A software package with modules that work independently and concurrently.

IP: *See* Transmission Control Protocol/Internet Protocol.

LAN: *See* local area network.

LM_NET: An Internet listserv for media specialists and librarians.

local area network (LAN): A set of interconnected hardware devices designed to share software and hardware peripherals. A LAN is usually confined to a fairly small geographical area—one building, or a group of buildings close to each other. LANs can be bridged to communicate with one another.

MAN: *See* metropolitan area network.

megabyte: One million bytes.

megaHertz (mHz): One million cycles per second. A unit of measurement used to indicate the clock speed of a computer microprocessor.

metropolitan area network (MAN): A district, region, or citywide network.

mHz: *See* megaHertz.

Microcomputer Library Interchange Format (MicroLIF): A standard established in 1987 by a group of library vendors to allow the exchange of MARC records in microcomputer-based automated systems. In 1991, this standard became known as U.S. MARC/MicroLIF

Protocol for its conformity with the Library of Congress U.S. MARC. *See also* U.S. MARC/MicroLIF Protocol.

MicroLIF: *See* Microcomputer Library Interchange Format.

microprocessor: A single chip containing the CPU.

module: A component of a software program that represents a function and performs the tasks associated with it.

nesting: A process of using parentheses around search statements when more than one Boolean operator exists. It is also referred to as nested logic. It is mainly used to instruct database retrieval software to follow the appropriate order of processing of Boolean operators.

Novell Netware: An IBM-compatible network operating system.

OCLC (Online Computer Library Center): A nationwide bibliographic utility used for resource sharing among libraries and other member institutions.

online public access catalog (OPAC): A part of an automation software used by patrons to find and retrieve information. It is equivalent to the card catalog.

OPAC: *See* online public access catalog.

operating system: Software that controls the computer's functions.

OSIRIS: A student record management system developed by McGraw-Hill School Systems. It is widely used in public schools in the state of Georgia.

PCI: See peripheral component interconnect.

peripheral component interconnect (PCI): A computer bus architecture currently used with Intel Pentium microprocessors.

Precision One: A CD-ROM database of MARC records developed by Brodart Automation. It is mainly used for retrospective conversion.

random access memory (RAM): A volatile memory in which programs are executed and data is processed. Unless the data is saved, it is destroyed when the computer is turned off.

RAM: *See* random access memory.

read-only memory (ROM): A permanent computer memory created during manufacturing. Data cannot be altered or erased.

Recon: *See* retrospective conversion.

repeater: A device used to connect one or more segments of a cable to re-amplify the signal received on one segment before it reaches the next segment, thus increasing the attenuation signal.

retrospective conversion: The process of converting a library's shelflist cards into a machine-readable format (i.e., U.S. MARC) that can be stored and retrieved by automation software.

ROM: *See* read-only memory.

SCSI: *See* small computer system interface.

Serial Line Internet Protocol/Point-to-Point Protocol (SLIP/PPP): Software that allows Internet access over a serial line or through a serial port. Commonly used with a modem connection.

server: *See* client-server.

shelflist: A section of a card catalog that contains a master copy of each cataloged item in a library's collection. Shelflist cards are usually filed by call number (e.g., Dewey Decimal, Library of Congress, etc.).

SLIP/PPP: *See* Serial Line Internet Protocol/Point-to-Point Protocol.

small computer system interface (SCSI) card: A card that can connect many hardware devices (e.g., CD-ROMs, hard disks, printers, scanners) to a computer using only one internal system slot.

stand-alone software: Nonintegrated software with modules that work independently of each other.

Telnet: A software program that allows remote login on the Internet.

TCP/IP: *See* Transmission Control Protocol/Internet Protocol.

Transmission Control Protocol/Internet Protocol: A set of two protocols used for all communications over the Internet.

U.S. MARC: *See* United States Machine-Readable Cataloging.

U.S. MARC/MicroLIF Protocol: A 1991 update to the standard MicroLIF. It is fully compatible with Library of Congress U.S. MARC.

Uniform Resource Locator (URL): A standard for specifying an Internet address, especially for sites on the World Wide Web.

uninterruptible power supply (UPS): A unit that keeps a file server running for a short time after a power shortage.

United States Machine-Readable Cataloging (U.S. MARC): A bibliographic standard for cataloging materials in automated systems. It allows the interchange of bibliographic information across automated systems. It is used and distributed by the Library of Congress.

UNIX: An interactive timesharing operating system. It is a trademark of AT&T Bell Laboratories. It runs on minicomputers and powerful microcomputers.

URL: *See* Uniform Resource Locator.

WAN: *See* wide area network.

wide area network (WAN): A statewide, regional, nationwide or worldwide network, for example, OCLC and the Internet.

World Wide Web (WWW): An Internet server that provides access to hyperlinked and graphical Internet resources.

WWW: *See* World Wide Web.

Z39.50: A standard that allows various computer systems to execute, search, retrieve, and display information in one common interface format, regardless of the hardware, software, database structure, or platform used. This standard is being implemented in many OPACs to facilitate their access on the World Wide Web.

Additional Readings

American National Standard Institute and National Information Standards Organization. 1995. *American National Standard Information Retrieval Application Service Definition and Protocol Specifications for Open Systems Interconnection.* (ANSI/NISO Z39.50.) Bethesda, MD: National Information Standards Office.

Adams, Helen. 1994. Media magic: Automating a K-12 library program in a rural district. *Emergency Librarian* 21 (May/June): 24–29.

Barger, Sherie. 1996. Technology and change. *Florida Media Quarterly* 21 (1): 58–59.

Bland, Kay P. 1996. School libraries reaching out: The wireless connection (wireless phones at Fuller Elementary School). *Arkansas Libraries* 53 (April): 8–10.

Blodgett, Teresa, and Judi Repman. 1995. The electronic school library resource center: Facilities planning for the new information technologies. *Emergency Librarian* 22 (Jan/Feb.): 26–30.

Breeding, Marshall. 1996. *Integrated library systems for PCs & PC networks: Descriptive and analytical reviews on the current products.* Medford, NJ: Information Today.

Buckland, Michael. 1992. *Redesigning library services: A manifesto.* Chicago: American Library Association.

Caffarella, Edward P. 1996. Techniques for increasing the efficiency of automated systems in school library media centers: Queue theory. *School Library Media Quarterly* 24 (Spring): 151–54.

Clyde, Laurel A. 1996. InfoTech: Generic software packages in school libraries. *Emergency Librarian* 23 (May/June): 51–53.

Cohen, Elaine. 1994. The architectural and interior design planning process. *Library Trends* 42 (Winter): 547–63.

Cooper, Michael D. 1996. *Design of library automation systems: File structures, data structures, and tools.* New York: John Wiley and Sons.

Crowe, Linda, and Jane Light. 1994. Desperately seeking a system. *Library Journal* 119 (October): 42–44.

Ekhaml, Liticia T., and Paul A. Ekhaml. 1995. Some questions and issues about school networking. *School Library Media Activities Monthly* 11 (March): 37–39.

Feldman, Susan E., and Larry Krumenaker. 1996. *The Internet at a glance.* Medford, NJ: Learned Information.

Gilster, Paul. 1995. *The new Internet navigator.* New York: John Wiley and Sons.

Hallmark, Julie, and Rebecca Garcia C. 1996. Training for automated systems in libraries: Views of library administrators and vendors. *Information Technology and Libraries* 15 (September): 151–63.

Held, Gilbert. 1996. *Local area network performance: Issues and answers.* New York: John Wiley and Sons.

Kessner, Richard. 1994. *Information systems: A strategic approach to planning and implementation.* Ann Arbor, MI: Books on Demand.

Krol, Ed. 1994. *The whole Internet: User's guide & catalog.* Sebastopol, CA: O'Reilly & Associates.

Kroll, Carol. 1994. Library media specialists move center stage: An example of implementation of information technologies. *School Library Media Annual* 12: 70–75.

Lankford, Mary D. 1994. Design for change: How to plan the school library you really need. *School Library Journal* 40 (February): 20–24.

LeLoup, Dennis. 1995. Finding funds to go high tech. *Technology Connection* 2 (May): 27–28.

Library Trends. Winter 1994. The entire issue is devoted to the topic, "Library finance: New needs, new models."

Lund, Jennifer. 1997. *Internet at a glance.* Reading, MA: Addison-Wesley.

Manczuk, Suzanne, and R. J. Pasco. 1994. Planning for technology: A newcomer's guide. *Journal of Youth Services in Libraries* 7 (Winter): 199–206.

Mather, Becky R. 1997. *Creating a local area network in the school library media center.* Westport, CT: Greenwood Publishing.

Metz, Ray E., and Gail Junion-Metz. 1996. *Using the World Wide Web & creating home pages: A how-to-do-it manual for librarians.* New York: Neal-Schuman.

Michael, James J., and Mark Hinnebusch. 1994. *From A to Z39.50: A networking primer.* Westport, CT: Mecklermedia.

Ogg, Harold C. 1997. *Introduction to the use of computers in libraries.* Medford, NJ: Learned Information.

———. 1995. *Introduction to the use of computers in libraries: A textbook for the non-technical student.* Medford, NJ: Learned Information.

Simpson, Carol M. 1995. *Internet for library media specialists.* Worthington, OH: Linworth.

Stallings, William. 1995. *The official Internet World Internet security handbook*. Westport, CT: Mecklermedia.

Swan, James. 1996. *Automating small libraries*. Fort Atkinson, WI: Highsmith Press.

———. 1996. Automating small libraries. *Rural Libraries* 16 (1): 7–22.

Tebbetts, Diane R. 1996. Global implications for local automation. *Microcomputers for Information Management* 13 (1): 31–40.

Thornton, Joyce K. 1995. Battling carpal tunnel syndrome through ergonomics: A case study of Texas A&M's library provides insights and answers. *Computers in Libraries* 15 (September): 22–25.

Wolfgram, Linda M. 1996. The effects of automation on school library media centers. *Journal of Youth Services in Libraries* 9 (Summer): 387–94.

Index